KU-791-345

Edited by Ian Luna

New New York
recent buildings in the city

Introduction by Joseph Giovannini

U.W.E.L
LEARNING RESOURCES
2298361   CLASS 071
CONTROL   720.
0500284547   97471
DATE   SITE
15. APR. 2004   WV   NEW

Thames & Hudson

Table of Contents

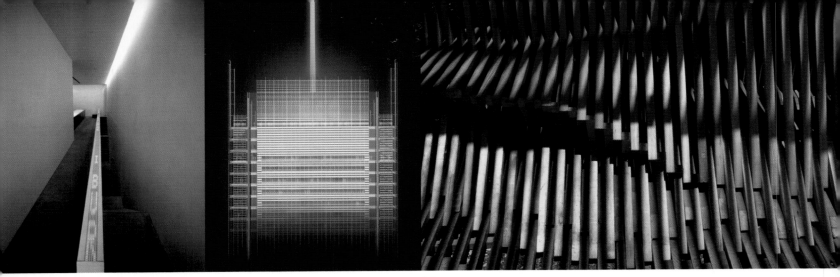

01.   02.   03.

New Yorkers are jaywalkers at heart and in practice, and it was only a matter of time before architects here would skip the constraining crosswalks laid out by postmodernists in the 1980s, when typologically correct tripartite buildings, with a base, middle and top, ruled the drafting boards. Apartment buildings in Battery Park City now being built still suffer from aesthetic covenants mandating the so-called New Yorkness of New York; design recipes perpetuate the ideology that this patch of Manhattan look and behave like the Upper East Side and West Side at the turn of the last century.

New New York: Architecture of a City offers encyclopedic evidence that news of the death of New York architecture by history has been greatly exaggerated. Over the last decade, designers have marched to their own drummers, moving beyond the blandishments of postmodernism and its covert reincarnation, the New Urbanism. Perhaps postmodernism offered insight as a critique of modernism's fault lines, but the linguistic premise that architectural postmodernism should be historicist, because of the "post," was a misconception. As Renzo Piano succinctly stated when he accepted the Pritzker Prize at the White House in 1998, looking to the past is not the way forward into the future. In a simple phrase, Piano dismissed an hour-long exhortation about tradition by Vincent Scully, a previous speaker that evening. Piano's own current proposal for the New York Times Tower (fig. 02) illustrates his position: the design does not recycle profiles from Central Park West or Rockefeller Center, but explores the potential of glass to redefine the skin of the high-rise as a set of gossamer veils; in an inversion of expectations unusual for a canonical modernist, surface supercedes structure as message.

If the architectural pulse of the city threw itself into reverse, toward the past, New York's volatile cultural metabolism could not sustain dwelling there; Manhattan society itself turns over every one or two decades, burning pedigrees faster than any other American city besides Hollywood.

Sitting on the volcano of its own ambition, New York is endlessly destabilized by the collective Vesuvian energies of its rampant strivers. After the momentous Deconstructivist Architecture Show at MoMA in 1988, which closed the curtain on postmodernism, numerous actors and agents converged as though in astronomical alignment to move New York's architectural position out of the stasis of history. Three or four architecture schools, several museum design departments, numerous nonprofit organizations, a large constellation of galleries, artists and museums, and New York design periodicals all constituted an intellectual motor driving the city's architectural ecosystem, and their synergy stirred and redefined praxis here even in the absence of a new reigning ideology. Just as the Italian government collapses periodically and runs remarkably well in the interregnum, architecture sometimes finds its own path spontaneously without the benefit of a definitive theory map.

Even in the 1980s, the boutique hotels that Andrée Putman and then Philippe Starck designed for Ian Schrager snatched attention away from the skyscrapers with the "hats," done by name-brand corporate architects. Putman's Morgan and then Starck's Royalton both exemplified the possibility of significant design at smaller scale by freethinking designers outside the commercial mainstream. Simultaneously, grass-roots patronage emerged for avantgarde design at an even smaller scale because of New York's loft phenomenon. New Yorkers are always renovating because of the turnover in apartments and stores, and like sands churning in the desert, changing Manhattan interiors has been a basis of practice for small and fledgling firms in a city where third- and fourth-generation buildings require a corporate hand. But for at least twenty-five years, lofts—where owners subscribing to alternative lifestyles required unconventional floor plans and images—have been petri dishes for experimentation. The idea of the loft even migrated uptown to traditional apartments in dowager buildings on the avenues.

New New York

Joseph Giovannini

Loft culture started going public in the mid-1980s, when restaurateurs opened big, roaring dining halls. Stores soon followed, in which large, open volumes offered the luxury of space. At the same time, the lofts in which artists had worked since the early days of SoHo spawned gallery equivalents, and these galleries dovetailed with the loft phenomenon well under way. Gluckman Mayner, architects of minimalist Dia Center for the Arts on 23rd Street, became early specialists in the discipline and art of well-lit cubic perfection in a string of galleries and stores. In the Gagosian Gallery, the Helmut Lang Parfumerie (fig. 01) and the Mary Boone Gallery, Gluckman Mayner have clearly been affected by the art their designs display, and though they were specialists in designing the vessel that held the art, the art itself played osmotically into their designs. The architects stripped down interiors to irreducible essences, much as Donald Judd did in his sculpture.

With the confluence of restaurants, stores and galleries, SoHo, TriBeCa and most recently Chelsea emerged as New York's most active architectural laboratory, shifting the center of design gravity out of MoMA's orbit, and away from the corporate vistas of new high-rise towers that, in a simulation of Houston, crisscrossed Midtown in the 1980s. First with the boutique hotels, and then with the loft phenomenon largely Downtown, a dispersive pattern of design loci emerged, which bypassed the central control that MoMA had always held since the International Style Show of 1932. Without any galvanizing shows to follow up the Deconstructivist exhibition, and especially with its own underwhelming design for the MoMA expansion by Yoshiko Taniguchi, MoMA ceded its leadership position to the simple momentum of a city that couldn't wait.

New York got design through a hundred points of light, through decentralization in galleries, restaurants, stores or apartment lofts, many displayed lavishly in the *New York Times*. MoMA became more conservative than the city itself, even though MoMA and its sister institution P. S. 1

cosponsored several strong installations at the Long Island City museum. During annual summer programs, the two institutions introduce emerging talents and topical issues. At the P. S. 1 courtyard, the curvilinear wood pavilions called Dunescape (fig. 03), created by SHoP with the help of a computer, and Lindy Roy's "SubWave," a conceptual environment of cooling mechanisms—wall fans, water atomizers and rotating, swinging hammocks—were both strong installations, but relegated to anecdotal status as summer amusements. Otherwise, MoMA's own symbolic effort at keeping up with the avant-garde fell short: the museum hired Los Angeles architect Michael Maltzan for its temporary digs at MoMA QNS, but stopped his rolling entrance topography at the doors of the galleries, as though design were a threat to art, rather than an environmental tool in explaining and enhancing it. MoMA has succeeded in missing its own design message. The city as a whole has spontaneously filled the breach.

Smaller, noninstitutional clients and private individuals, their eyes trained in the sophisticated New York visual environment, drew on one of the largest talent banks in the world. The boutique patronage encouraged practices that do not operate on the corporate model; by a process of spontaneous inversion, the large corporate firms that had defined the agenda in the 1980s were marginalized as New York's defining practices, while boutique firms came out of the margins, surprised to find themselves at the center. Sensing the displacement, corporate firms have in some cases developed semiautonomous studios within their design pen, to encourage signature work that would break the corporate stamp. Or they have hired designers out of their own independent practices to reinvigorate their design departments. Skidmore, Owings & Merrill, for example, now designs with environmental artists integrated in the project from design inception. The vector of even corporate operations points to a search for voice.

04. 05. 06. 07.

If there is a centrism to the hundred points of light, a magnetic pull unifying the designs, it may be the pervasive influence of art as a way of understanding and creating architecture. Once a literary city with a spiritual center in the Village, New York has become a city in which the eye has trumped the word as the dominant cultural force: New Yorkers are so sensitized to art, installations, galleries and museums that they expect architecture, when practiced at its best, to be an art. As art, however, buildings could not be conventional in the way postmodernists espoused architecture as a discipline evolving within its own tradition. Nor could architecture be neutral and dispassionate in its functional objectivity, as early adherents of the Bauhaus advocated. In the 1990s, art impregnated architecture as an ideal and practice, necessitating that each artist-architect cultivate signature forms and concepts. The architecture could not be derivative; originality, rather than schools codifying design, defined identity.

Inspired by Richard Serra's *Torqued Ellipses*, Studio Morsa and Takao Kawasaki, for example, designed a swirling configuration of clothing displays in Comme des Garçons on West 22nd Street in Chelsea, a couple of doors away from where Serra's steel vortices had been exhibited at Dia Center for the Arts. In Tribeca, at the Issey Miyake boutique, Frank Gehry, with his son Alejandro, unfurled ribbons of stainless steel through a space designed by associated architect Gordon Kipping. Gehry was using his Bilbao language of streaming form. At Issey Miyake Pleats Please, Toshiko Mori essentially created an art installation, with a brilliantly colored check-out cube floating in a luminous space viewed through a film applied to the plate-glass windows that optically shifted the interior from pellucid clarity to blur as a viewer browsed the store from the outside.

Once a downtown denizen, Marcel Duchamp has left a lasting imprint on the New York artistic psyche, and his long shadow can be felt in the incisive yet insouciant works of Diller+Scofidio, architects who design conceptual commentaries in built form. In their redesign of the Brasserie in the Seagrams Building, diners at the door make their "entrance" by camera on video screens projected into the dining area before they sweep down the stairs. Blurred glass fuzzes wine labels on the racks behind the bar, simulating inebriation before the fact. In their winning scheme for the Eyebeam Museum (fig. 05), the architects loop a double highway ramping up some ten stories in a promenade whose contours bend space; with its overlooks and cornerless geometry, the interactive building prompts people to explore every fold in the urban journey. Like sculptors who long ago abandoned the stand-alone object, the architects deobjectify the building and turn it into open form encouraging raw experience.

Equivalent pluck is displayed by the architects of Lot/ek, an Italian group practicing in New York, which retrieves abandoned iceboxes, kitchen sinks and other discarded industrial body parts from the dumpster. In the Miller/Jones Studio, the architects salvaged one side of a 40-foot-long aluminum shipping container, and adapted the wall, complete with patina, as a Duchampian *objet trouvé* dividing the loft. Also in Duchamp's gently wicked spirit, Thomas Leeser turned the facade of the Glass Bar (fig. 04) into a voyeuristic performance piece by siting the washbasin of the unisex lavatory at the front facade, behind a one-way mirror; customers primp in front of a passing streetside audience they can't see. In New York, conceptual art became the catalyst for spaces that fused art, fashion, architecture and shopping in a kind of urban performance dissolving distinctions between high and low.

More conceptual than retinal, the work of these architects represents a radical shift from modernism's classic interest in abstractions of space, light and form. If concept is not physical and formal, the architects still achieve proprietary claim over their ideas by slanting the concepts so uniquely that they acquire fingerprints, becoming, effectively, intellectual property. As in the art world, identity became foundational

08.

09.

in New York architecture. Few works in this book are derivative, unless they evolve from precedents established by the same architect.

In this always-entrepreneurial city, originality was pressed into commercial duty, entering the equation of how an entrepreneur creates and markets a brand. Moving beyond minimalism and heading toward media performance, Prada hired Rem Koolhaas to fashion its Epicenter store in New York in the same way the Guggenheim, under the corporate management of Tom Krens, used design to develop the Guggenheim as a brand. The New York-based Guggenheim virtually invented the concept of destination architecture via Frank Lloyd Wright and then Frank Gehry, and the so-called Bilbao effect has rebounded on New York, turning shops, galleries, boutiques, restaurants, large and small, into destination spots with local, regional and even international reach. No single design cultivated cultural blur better than Prada, which combined living theater, performance and heavy doses of public relations. At its epic opening, thousands of guests, including Mayor Giuliani—all wearing admissions bracelets—signaled the emergence of loft culture as a mainstream phenomenon. Prada was selling Koolhaas while Koolhaas was selling concept.

To be sure, several unreconstructed modernists survived postmodernism. Richard Meier and Charles Gwathmey, who already had a strong signature in the 1970s, simply maintained and refined it. Meier recently completed the elegant, twinned Perry Steet Towers on the waterfront in the West Village, a crisply framed, beautifully detailed and diaphanous pair of apartment buildings. Gwathmey, at the International Center of Photography and the New York Public Library, Science, Industry and Business Library, produced strong, volumetric interiors clearly based on his early work. However, a breakout design, with a distorted top for an addition to the New York Public Library, was forced and exaggerated, and less successful than his characteristic work. Synonymous with high tech, Sir Norman Foster created

a tower for the Hearst corporation featuring a woven lattice acting as a steel exoskeleton. The Polshek Partnership adapted high tech to eighteenth-century rationalism in the Rose Center for Earth and Space, with a monumental globe suspended in a perfect glass cube, a design inspired by architect Claude-Nicholas Ledoux. With the demise of post-modernism, this kind of modernism came to represent a conservative ideology, known and practiced for years. When MoMA produced the Taniguchi scheme, architecture historian Victoria Newhouse noted in her book, *The New Museum*, that the design could have been conceived in the 1940s. The modernism was comfortable and appealing for eyes that had grown up at MoMA.

This cool, rationalist form of modernism, however, was ceding ground to a more expressive modernism; early Le Corbusier and the Bauhaus were giving way at last to a tradition of warmer, more humanistic modernism, which had been practiced by Eero Saarinen in such structures as the TWA building at John F. Kennedy Airport. In one of the city's new crop of signal works, Tod Williams and Billie Tsien designed the American Folk Art Museum (fig. 06), whose subtly nuanced interiors, with shadowy moments ceding to generous natural light, represented a moody building tending to subjectivity rather than objectivity. The Austrian Cultural Forum, by Raymond Abraham, was more than moody. It was brooding with its darkly dangerous facade poised over the street like the blade of a guillotine. Rafael Viñoly, at the Physical Education Facility of Lehman College, took this kind of expressive modernism into thematic metaphor, with an athletic-looking gym, its roof vaulting through the air in a long, free-span leap.

Skidmore, Owings & Merrill, smelling the coffee, revinvented itself in a single design, the spectacular Daniel Patrick Moynihan Station (fig. 07), where a space frame, curved like a section of a sphere, defined the public space breaking the main classical building from the train shed behind. In Four Times Square, a tower that forms a gateway into

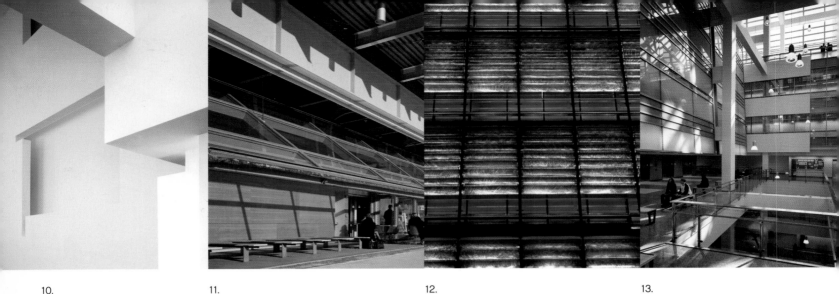

10. 11. 12. 13.

Times Square, Fox and Fowle pieced together a convincing collage of buildings that represents the multiple natures of its immediate context—monumental and showy, distinguished and rowdy. The tower culminates in a high-tech crown.

Despite their corporate provenance and purpose, the designs managed to import the design intensity of small projects to a large scale. All these buildings opened the expressive range of buildings in New York that had been too long restricted by reductive ideology received from early modernism.

The deconstructivist moment was never eclipsed but after its spectacular debut simply proceeded under the quieter, more academic rubric of poststructuralism. In the swerve away from the objectivity of modernism's scientific character, the poststructuralist architects no longer pledge allegiance to structure, having lost belief in structure as a foundational truth. In his Staten Island Institute of the Arts and Sciences (fig. 08), a building with walls and floors turning like ribbons in continuous movement, Peter Eisenman improved on Gehry by making the entire building flow, not just the facade; the interior was not a configuration of adapted boxes, like many of Gehry's interiors, nor was it simply extruded, as in many of Eisenman's previous designs. Polshek, whose partners produce widely varying designs, created a new entrance for the Brooklyn Museum of Art, fragmenting the notion of a heroic flight of classicized stairs with a fanning geometry interrupted by diverse elements of the program—entrance, sitting park, tickets, performance space.

Parisian architect Christian de Portzamparc also used fracture to achieve a strange harmony in the LVMH—Louis Vuitton-Möet Hennessy—Tower (fig. 09). Portzamparc broke the facade into facets that he set obliquely to the street, to avoid reflecting the dark IBM building opposite. The architect frosted the white-water glass so that the snowy surfaces wouldn't catch the ominously dark building. Portzamparc

dared base the concept not on structure but on reflections, light, translucency and transparency.

For a number of architects, light—perhaps the ultimate poststructuralist material—was a new foundation on which to predicate design. Steven Holl constructed the offices of the D. E. Shaw & Company on glow (fig. 10), and the epiphany of the New 42nd Street Studios (fig. 12), by Platt Byard Dovell White, was a facade of changing light, like a luminous and constantly changing Rothko canvas.

Other architects used other immaterialities. Henry Smith-Miller and Laurie Hawkinson, at the Wall Street Ferry Terminal (fig. 11), and Lewis Tsurumaki Lewis, at the Van Alen Institute, created operable building parts that transform their respective spaces through interactivity. The buildings are negotiable, structured on the notion of change. The entire facade of Steven Holl's Storefront for Art and Architecture pivots, changing its character from closed to open, opaque to porous.

In Lerner Hall at Columbia University (fig. 14), Bernard Tschumi expanded the primary suspended, plate-glass facade with switchback ramps, effectively creating a shadow theater for students plying a facade acting as a propylaeum to their mailboxes on the upper floors. Activity and movement rather than structure are the building block that defined the meaning of a building that looked deceptively high-tech. At Baruch College (fig. 13), William Pedersen, of Kohn Pedersen Fox, opened up the interior section of the block-long behemoth to create a vertical campus, its landings teeming with students. Space was designed to socialize students in this otherwise tight urban location.

The computer confirmed the poststructuralist search for an architectural approach beyond structure as a totalizing force. A younger generation of digital architects started thinking on, and with, the computer, using animation soft-ware that produced curviplanar forms very difficult to draw

14.   15.

and conceive by hand. Architects were visualizing surfaces rather than structure; the plan was no longer the generator. A consortium of architects practicing in different cities— Greg Lynn, Douglas Garofalo and Michael McInturf— designed the Korean Presbyterian Church in Queens (fig. 15), one of the first buildings to be wholly conceived and executed on the computer. Architect Winka Dubbeldam folded the facade of a mixed-used loft building on Greenwich Street in Manhattan, while SHoP enlisted the logarithmic intelligence of a computer to generate a facade for MoSex, a museum of sex with a thematically curvaceous skin. In both designs, continuously differentiated exterior surfaces superceded structure, though the facades, finally, made little impact on the striated floor organization inside.

If New York architecture is generally flourishing at a small or intermediate scale, with occasional examples of excellence at a large scale, it is because the age of Jane Jacobs has superceded that of Robert Moses, and shows no sign of releasing its grip. Had Westway been built, New Yorkers would now be basking on the Hudson, but that mighty project was defeated by local activists, and New Yorkers now must contend with fjording a high speed artery masked as an avenue, to gain access to the well-intended but limited recreational patches and strips of the Hudson River Park, which borders the Hudson up to 59th Street. The city has been unable to work with New Jersey to shape the design of the shared riverfront and harbor, which are being nibbled away by scores of independent projects rather than supporting a larger vision. Similarly, 42nd Street was resurrected like a Phoenix, but despite two impeccable theater restorations by Hardy Holzman Pfeiffer and the New 42nd Street Studios, the quality of the architecture, including the Westin New York Hotel by Arquitectonica, is wildly uneven and sometimes cartoonish. Robert Stern, one of the coordinators officiating over the design, mistakes New York for Disneyland, and steers the street toward theme design.

But nowhere is the city's inability to think large so manifest as at the World Trade Center, a parcel fraught by a tragedy whose difficulties were compounded by the Balkanizing control of too many clients, including Port Authority, the city, the state and not least, the developer, Larry Silverstein. In the spirit of showing what the projects might be, Herbert Muschamp in the *New York Times Magazine* and this critic, in *New York* magazine, independently organized a group of architects who offered alternatives to those first presented by Beyer Blinder Bell. The city, critics felt, deserved better than what was being offered.

The Port Authority and the Lower Manhattan Development Corporation finally staged an international competition for architects, and the finalists did indeed produce several viable schemes—notably, Norman Foster's inspired reinterpretation of the Twin Towers as a turning, kissing pair of environmentally intelligent twins, and Daniel Libeskind's winning entry, whose angular geometries derived from the event itself and mystified the buildings through surface graphics. A consortium of young architects, United, produced an unprecedented reinvention of the high-rise typology, with turning towers that met and morphed in public spaces reclaimed in the Manhattan stratosphere. Governor Pataki, finally, decided in favor of the Libeskind scheme, partially because the architect gave up design control of the ten million square feet of office space in favor of memorial buildings of his invention.

The glory of architecture in this city of historically huge projects and large vision now resides at a surprisingly small scale. The rampant multiplicity of unleashed voices refuses to be homogenized by a single, correct way of thinking, and even though each architect is on her own, together they have achieved critical mass. Architecture in New York is still delirious.

Joseph Giovannini

Selected Projects

01.

02.

Whitehall Ferry Terminal Peter Minuit Park

Whitehall and South streets
Schwartz Architects
2004

Integral to New York City's critical infrastructure, the Whitehall Ferry Terminal on the southeastern tip of Manhattan serves the 70,000 commuters who daily negotiate the 25-minute trip to and from Staten Island. Mirrored by St. George's Terminal on the Staten Island side, the port and the boats that use its three slips are managed by the New York City Department of Transportation (DOT). Originally built in 1907, the facility underwent significant renovation in the 1950s, but was damaged by fire in 1991. A competition for a new terminal was held the following year by the New York City Economic Development Corporation. The brief required the replacement of the building, a seismic refit of the rotted pile foundation underneath it, and the addition of a new landscaped court that marks the intermediate space between Battery Park and the East River esplanade. The implementation was to be phased as the ferry service had to operate through construction.

Venturi, Scott Brown & Associates (VSBA) and Schwartz Architects submitted the competition-winning entry—a scheme dominated by an enormous clock—but was rejected by Staten Island officials. The city reduced the scope of the project substantially after 1994, and with the withdrawal of VSBA, Frederic Schwartz was retained to devise a consensus builder. From the outset, the design was subject to a complicated review and oversight process, through a bureaucratic tangle rivaled only by the sequence of underpasses, water mains, power lines and the subway lines that undergird the site. With direct funding from federal, state, city and private corporate sources, the team had to manage a number of competing interests and marked pauses in funding before constructing began in earnest in 2000.

Frederic Schwartz substituted the rotund, mid-century pavilion with a glass wedge that sweeps landward to the stone-paved forecourt of Peter Minuit Park. The glass-and-steel building is supported on the water by a massive, triple-sleeve caisson foundation, and sits to the east of the historic Battery Maritime Building. Altogether, the project comprises 225,000 square-feet of program. The light-filled, 75-foot-high waiting room is augmented by east and west exiting concourses, a main entry hall, a food court, offices for the DOT, and an observation deck with extensive views of the harbor beyond.

The project's environmental agenda employs a building-integrated photovoltaic system that will relieve a portion of the building's energy requirement, with the solar panels mounted along the steel canopy that hangs over the viewing deck. The plan restores the tidal wetline with marsh grass, and additional plantings are proposed to fully transform the concrete surface of the former Peter Minuit Plaza into Peter Minuit Park.

01. View of the Whitehall Street entry and the taxi and bus drop-off.

02. The distinctive paving pattern of the new Peter Minuit Park is visible in this aerial montage of lower Manhattan.

03. Second floor plan.

03.

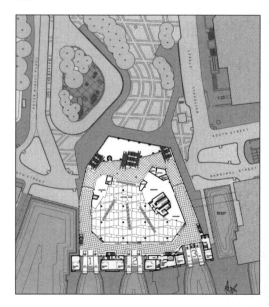

15

04.

05.

06.

04. Section looking west.

05. Whitehall Street facade, under construction.

06. Ferry slips, under construction. LED panels are suspended over the docks.

07. Perspective rendering: The renovation of the concrete caissons required significant marine engineering from Robert Silman Associates. Other features include a reinforced bulkhead and the reuse of existing slip and relieving platforms, gallows and machinery for ferry boarding ramps, piles and grade beams.

07.

Wall Street Ferry Terminal

Pier 11
Smith-Miller + Hawkinson
2000

This project is part of a long-term project initiated by the New York City Economic Development Corporation and the New York City Department of Transportation to promote the use of inter-borough ferry services and enhance public access to the Lower Manhattan waterfront facing the East River. Upgrading the Wall Street and East River esplanades mandated improvements to Pier 11, a historic wharf extending from Gouverneur Lane, one block south of Wall Street. The New York firm of Henry Smith-Miller and Laurie Hawkinson was selected to design the waiting terminal and barge canopies atop the pier in collaboration with the maritime and structural engineering services of Arup. The new Wall Street Ferry Terminal services the water taxis arriving from Brooklyn, Queens, New Jersey and the three area airports. The building is intended to provide a seamless transition between interior and exterior, land and sea.

The 2,100-square-foot terminal supports waiting, retail, office and storage areas. The huge glass doors on the east and west elevation function much like those in airplane hangars. In winter, the doors swing shut to enclose the terminal, and in summer, they serve as canopies, affording significant shade.

As an extension of the esplanade, the terminal serves both commuter and visitors. Amenities like the indoor/outdoor cafe are intended to attract people who work and live in the community, particularly in the warmer months.

The building materials include galvanized corrugated metal, corrugated fiberglass, non-relfective glass, and exposed structural steel; all materials reference waterfront construction and evoke the industrial past of New York's docks.

01. Along the Wall Street esplanade, Pier 11 commands views of Brooklyn and New York harbor.

02.

03.

02. Ferry slips project along the length of a
covered walkway.

03. - 05. The waiting areas are shielded by a
huge, operable glass door on the south-facing
side, which swings open in the warmer months.

01.

02.

03.

04.

NYSE Advanced Command Center
NYSE 3DTF

20 Broad Street
Asymptote
1999

In 1999, Hani Rashid and Lise Anne Couture of Asymptote executed two projects for the New York Stock Exchange. The first project is the design of a new Advanced Command Center situated within NYSE's Broad Street address; the second is a virtual-reality trading floor—displayed on an array of large flat-screen monitors—that enables viewers to oversee all activity in the exchange room.

Arranged along a 40-foot wall, the new command center integrates the virtual exchange model and interface into the exchange. Dubbed the "Ramp," the new resource affirms the 200-year-old institution's demonstrated capacity to incorporate the latest technologies—and is a fitting stage for media events conducted from the trading floor.

The principal design feature is a broad expanse of curvilinear blue glass. Described by the architects as "a physical analog to the movement and continuous flow of data and information throughout the space of the NYSE," the glazed wall is backlit, braced by a horizontal steel framework, and wired to supply data to an array of seventy high-resolution flat-screen monitors—including the nine screens that display the virtual trading floor. Equipped with plug-and-play capability, the individual components of the display wall can be manipulated to support a number of configurations.

01. - 03. In its debut, the Ramp, which supports the 3DTF, showcased six graphic visualization supercomputers, 43 high-resolution, flat-panel monitors and a custom application code. The curvature of the glass and accompanying double-curved work surface, the floating plasma monitors, and embedded message boards in the surrounding surfaces all create an illusion of a seamless and smooth space.

04. The backlit display featuring the NYSE logo.

05.

06.

10

07.

The 3DTF virtual trading floor was conceived as a digital refinement of the physical exchange. A wire-frame model that approximates the existing trading floor and its constituent parts was developed. This ideal environment had to be inherently flexible, able to parse large quantities of data efficiently, and adjust to changes in scale, levels of detail and the addition of a variety of virtual objects. Improving on the brick-and-mortar exchange, the virtual model functioned in real time: relative to the large amount of information it had to process and render, it required very little physical space. As portrayed by Asymptote, the project takes full advantage of opportunities in virtual space to transform spatial and temporal dimensions: "The 3DTF allows one to occupy several virtual spaces, scales, and points of view simultaneously. Captured events can also be instantly replayed alongside real-time events, and the user is able to compress, stretch, distort, or overlap these as required. The project posed an interesting opportunity to reconsider the 'reality' of the actual trading floor: although virtual and not intended to be constructed outside of a computer environment, [it] is effectively a direction for possible future trading environments. The virtual trading floor as designed, is both a reflection of the existing environment and a provocation for a new, physically augmented architecture."

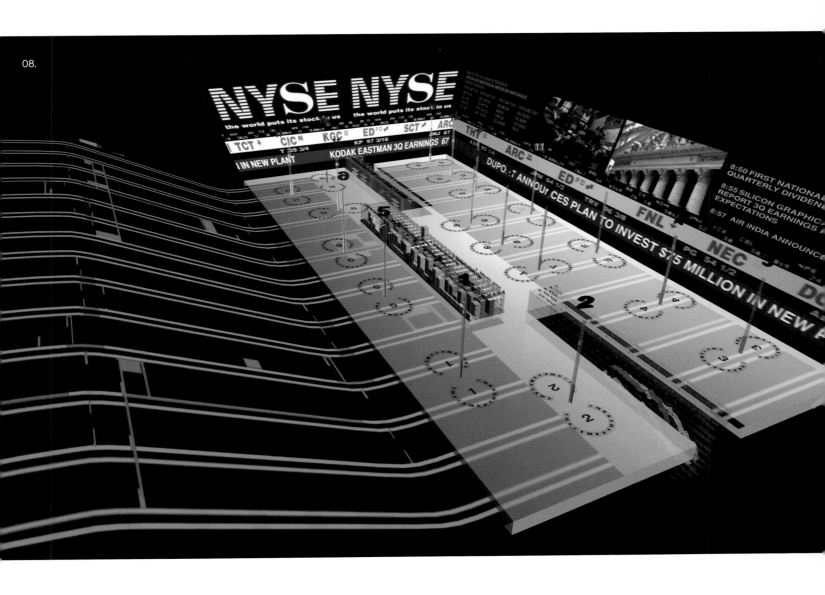

05. - 08. Visualizations of the trading spaces
created within the 3DTF.

01.

02.

Storefront for Art & Architecture

97 Kenmare Street
Steven Holl Architects & Vito Acconci
1993

Nearly four years after collaborating on a 1988 urban plan for an arts community in downtown Washington D. C., Steven Holl and artist Vito Acconci were commissioned by Kyong Park and Shirin Neshat of the Storefront for Art and Architecture to renovate one of a handful of exhibition spaces in the city that regularly feature the work of emerging architects. The gallery is situated on the corner of Kenmare and Centre Street, at a point where Chinatown, Little Italy and SoHo converge. The gallery occupies a triangular footprint, and its main external feature is a south-facing storefront along Kenmare Street.

Like the growth rings of a tree, the innumerable textural effects and layers of paint that participating architects had applied on the surface of the building exterior chronicled the exhibitions held at the site. Drawing from this accreted history, neither Acconci nor Holl were concerned with devising a permanent or static facade, much less a conventional exhibition program.

Puncturing the facade, the provisional design team proposed a challenge to the symbolic and literal enclosures that gird New York art by uniting the interior and exterior into a mutable architectural gesture. Using a hybrid material comprised of concrete mixed with recycled fibers, its creators injected a spirit of whimsy, inserting a series of hinged panels arranged in a puzzle-like configuration. When the panels are locked in their open position, the facade dissolves and the interior space of the gallery expands out onto the sidewalk.

01. - 02. Panels open onto Kenmare Street.

03. Northeast corner, Kenmare and Centre streets.

03.

05

04. - 06. Detail views. Swinging on hinges, the
operable panels are clad in a hybrid of
concrete and recycled flooring riveted onto
a steel frame.

01.

01. Interior view.

02. Exterior view, northwest corner.

03. Ground floor plan.

02.

Skyscraper Museum

39 Battery Place
Skidmore, Owings & Merrill
2003 Completion

In 2003, the Skyscraper Museum relocated to a storefront location in Battery Park City. (Through September 11, 2001, it occupied an interim location on 110 Maiden Lane.) Designed by Roger Duffy of Skidmore, Owings & Merrill, the museum incorporates its holdings at the foot of the new 38-story Ritz-Carlton Downtown Hotel by Gary Handel and Polshek Partnership, hemmed into the apex of a triangle formed by Battery Place to the west and First Place to the north.

Established in 1996 by historian Carol Willis, the Skyscraper Museum is the only one of its type devoted exclusively to the study of tall buildings, and the schematic concept suggested the integration of two "museums": the actual repository for artifacts and the fabric of the city itself. The exhibition program is intended to draw inspiration from the creative energy of New York City, the world's preeminent vertical metropolis. This dialogue is continued as objects from the permanent

and temporary collections are distributed to other sites within the "living museum": material of historical relevance to the development of the high-rise building type is placed in skyscrapers throughout Manhattan. This broad definition of "exhibition space" permits the institution to exceed its small enclosure.

Announced by a boldfaced, stainless steel inlay along the Battery Place sidewalk, the project consists of 5,800 square-feet of exhibition program, including a fully accessible 1,000-square-foot mezzanine level. Objects from the history of the skyscraper are enclosed in fourteen full-height vitrines, which are mirrored up and down in an infinite optical conceit by stainless steel panels mounted on both floor and ceiling. The sequence of reflection and distortion commences with the entrance canopy, a cube of clear glass and polished metal panels stretched over a steel frame that gestures to the street, as it asserts a formal identity distinct from its parent tower.

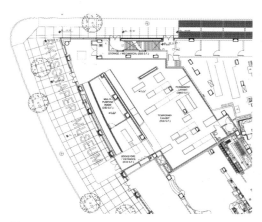

03.

01.

01. The Port Authority of New York and New Jersey commissioned Goshow Architects to design two parallel walkways leading to the ventilation shafts of the Holland Tunnel. The north access is strictly for emergency use, while the other is open for public use.

02. - 03. The completed greenspaces of Battery Park City, while outside the remit of the Hudson River Park Trust, are linked to the proposed new park areas. View looking out to New Jersey from Demetri Porphyrios' *Pavilion* (1992) inside Nelson Rockefeller Park.

Hudson River Park

Battery Place to 59th Street
Phase 1: 2003 Completion

In 1998, Governor George Pataki signed into law the creation of a verdant promenade along the West Side Highway. Adapted from a number of land-use proposals developed by the New York State Department of Transportation that date back to the early 1970s, and managed by a public trust accountable to both city and state, Hudson River Park represents the most extensive open-space development in Manhattan since Central Park. With some of its elements already in place, the new park extends nearly five miles from 59th Street to the southwestern tip of the island. While the project technically excludes the 92 acres under the Battery Park City Authority, it is physically connected to Robert F. Wagner Jr. Park and Rockefeller Park, two large recreational spaces between historic Castle Clinton and Chambers Street that were fully realized in the early to mid 1990s.

Hudson River Park incorporates nearly 500 acres of waterfront and limits commercial uses to less than twenty percent. Utilizing artifacts from the city's maritime past, much of the project will be built on the series of piers that collectively form the western spine of Manhattan. The ongoing construction program is divided into six segments—numbered 2 to 7—and the design and planning contracts within each segment are apportioned to a host of practices. Once completed, the park will feature a wide mix of active and passive recreational zones dotting the length of the waterside esplanade, and atop a dozen rehabilitated and publicly accessible piers that are expected to grow in number. In addition, the entire pierhead line and all inter-

pier marine environments have been designated as the Hudson River Estuarine Sanctuary. Three docks on the park Piers 26, 40 and 63—have been set apart for recreational use of the river by canoe and kayak, and are part of a water trail that starts at the mouth of New York Harbor and continues far up the Hudson.

Segments 2 and 3 of the park begin as a bike and footpath on Battery Place, the first mile of the Hudson River Valley Greenway Trail—which will one day stretch north all the way to Albany and Troy. Also in this section are Piers 25 and 26 on No. Moore Street, which now host skate ramps, a miniature golf course and marina; and Pier 34, with two concrete walkways connected to the ventilation shafts of the Holland Tunnel.

Above Canal Street to 14th Street, the Greenwich Village portion (segment 4) includes proposed sports facilities for Pier 40, lawns for sunbathing and play on Piers 45 and 46, and a water park for children on Pier 51 and Jane Street. Built on landfill, the Gansevoort Peninsula will become a sunbathing beach with real sand. Pier 53, the only remaining waterside firehouse will continue as the base of NYFD Marine Company One. Pier 54, the New York berth of the Cunard-White Star ocean liners (including the doomed *Lusitania*) will again host historic vessels, and accommodate a large concert venue. The landside plots are variously reserved for an entry sequence on Christopher Street complete with watercourses, a dog run at Leroy Street and a food court on Charles and Perry streets.

Segment 5 commences just above 14th Street to 26th Street, spanning Chelsea Piers (from Piers 59-62), Basketball City on Pier 63, and Chelsea Waterside. Inland, the triangle formed by Chelsea Waterside East supports a playground, basketball court, dog run, seating, and lawns. The Baltimore and Ohio Railroad Float on Pier 66A was recently restored, fitted with railings and is now open to the public.

Segment 6 encompasses a 33-block portion of upper Chelsea and lower Clinton from about 26th Street to 44th Street. The area from 27th to 37th streets is planned as an ecological habitat with facilities for the management of the Hudson River Estuarine Sanctuary. Ongoing negotiations for a stadium between 30th and 34th streets have left plans open for the rotted piles of Pier 72 and the immediate area, but a rocky beach is intended south of Pier 76 (displacing the NYPD tow yard), and a major civic gesture replete with fountains and a plaza is planned near 42nd Street. With the commercial port facilities from 38th to 44th still active, the open space of Pier 84 will be landscaped to integrate the area with the Park.

The principal feature proposed for the seventh, final segment is the Clinton Cove Park between the Passenger Ship Terminal on Piers 88-92 and the New York City Sanitation Marine Transfer Station on Pier 99 and 59th Street. A boathouse and amenities for sports and relaxation are envisaged for Piers 95-97.

01. - 02. Model of
titanium sculpture.

03. - 08. Installation of
titanium sheets.

09. Ground floor plan.

10. Cellar plan.

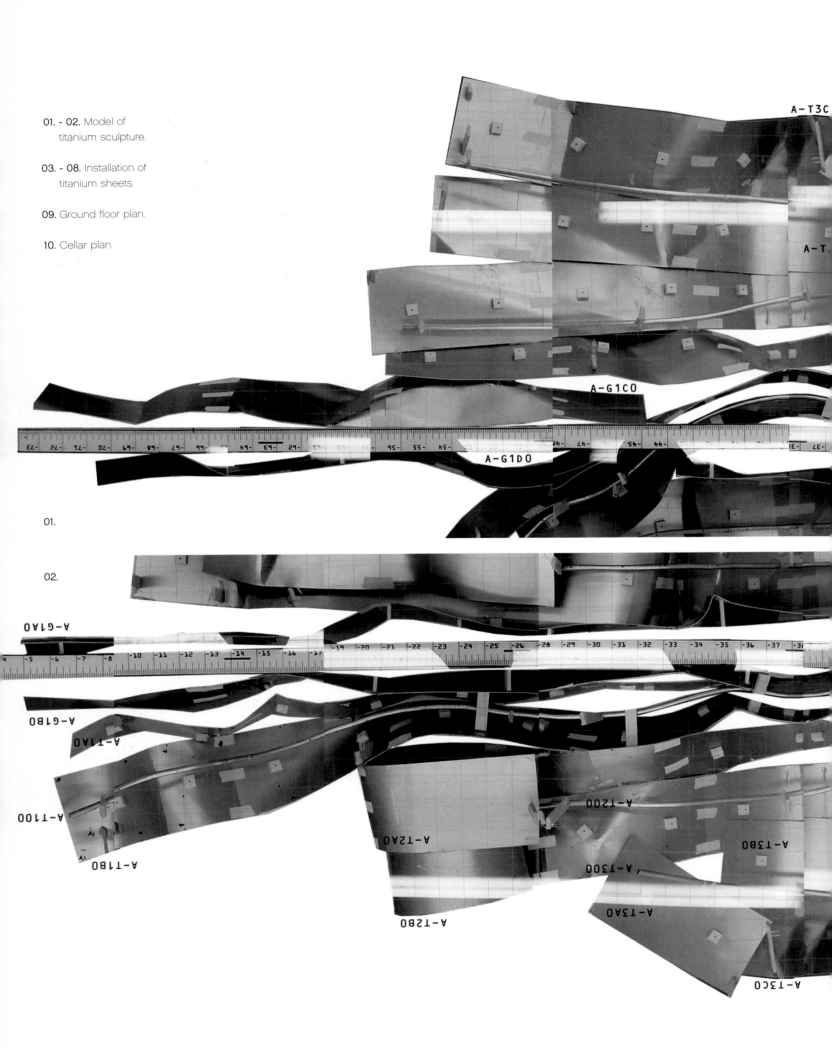

01.

02.

Issey Miyake Tribeca

119 Hudson Street
Frank O. Gehry & Gordon Kipping of GTECTS
2002

Issey Miyake is one of a select group of influential Japanese couturiers who in the 1990s, was most responsible for the transformation of the boutique from a strict retail type into an event-generator. Miyake conceived his emporia as venues where shopping can sometimes appear to be subordinate to other cultural uses—all of which, not incidentally, contribute to the promotion of a global brand. In his New York flagship, Miyake sought to export the narrative of surprise achieved by his previous architectural collaborations, most notably in Tokyo and Paris.

The Tribeca shop grew out of several visits the designer made to Frank Gehry's Santa Monica studio. A showcase for Issey Miyake Men's and Women's collections, Pleats Please, and for the A-POC (A Piece of Cloth) and Haat lines, the store also houses the new Issey Miyake USA headquarters. Miyake

described his vision of a "Gehry tornado" at the core of the space, uniting the individual sensibilities of the designer and architect into a wild, shimmering dance. Gehry agreed to sign on in tandem with Gordon Kipping of the New York firm GTECTS, who, in turn, was ultimately responsible for developing and executing the 14,600-square-foot retail, showroom and office program.

Fashioned out of titanium sheet, the sculpture emerges from the cellar level and whips through the main retail floor. As it rises, the unruly mass threatens to tear out the exposed wood lath structure of the ceiling. But the surface conceit of a violent, meteorological phenomenon belies a sectional delicacy: Joined to a hollow steel skeleton by velcro-baked neoprene disks, the ultra-thin sheets are themselves attached to each other by industrial Scotch tape.

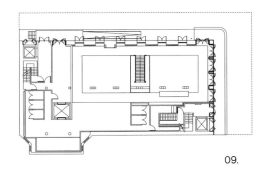

09.

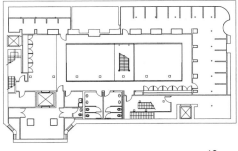

10.

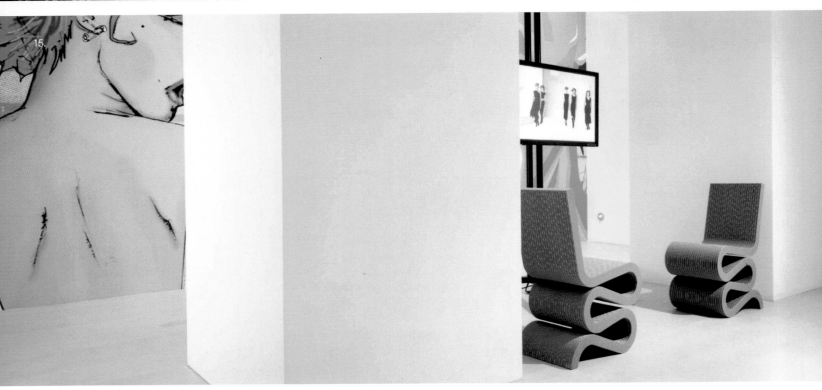

11. GTECTS directed the restoration of the original warehouse, designed by Thomas R. Jackson, in 1888. The cast iron facade was stripped to a bare metal finish and sealed clear.

12. - 14. Views of the titanium sheets on the ceiling. The system of neoprene discs supporting the individual sheets are visible.

15. Murals by Alejandro Gehry, within a space littered with his father's corrugated cardboard chairs.

Consistent with the idea of an ever-changing destination where visitors are surprised on each visit, the gallery displays a rotating display of work by young artists.

16. Stainless-steel stock cabinets along merchandise wall.

17. View looking down the shaft leading to the cellar level, where the showroom and corporate offices for Miyake USA are located.

18. - 19. Views of the cellar level showroom and retail area. Clothing racks, with oversized casters and stainless-steel rods, playfully mimic their Seventh Avenue precedents. The extensive use of glass permitted spatial and programmatic connections where they would not have otherwise been possible due to security concerns and vertical separation. The removal of the original wood plank flooring to reveal the original structure facilitated the insertion of a new glass box onto the cellar floor. The exposed joists supporting the ceiling are visible from above, through a five-foot-wide border of glass flooring on the main floor.

20. Sketch of the "tornado" by Frank Gehry.

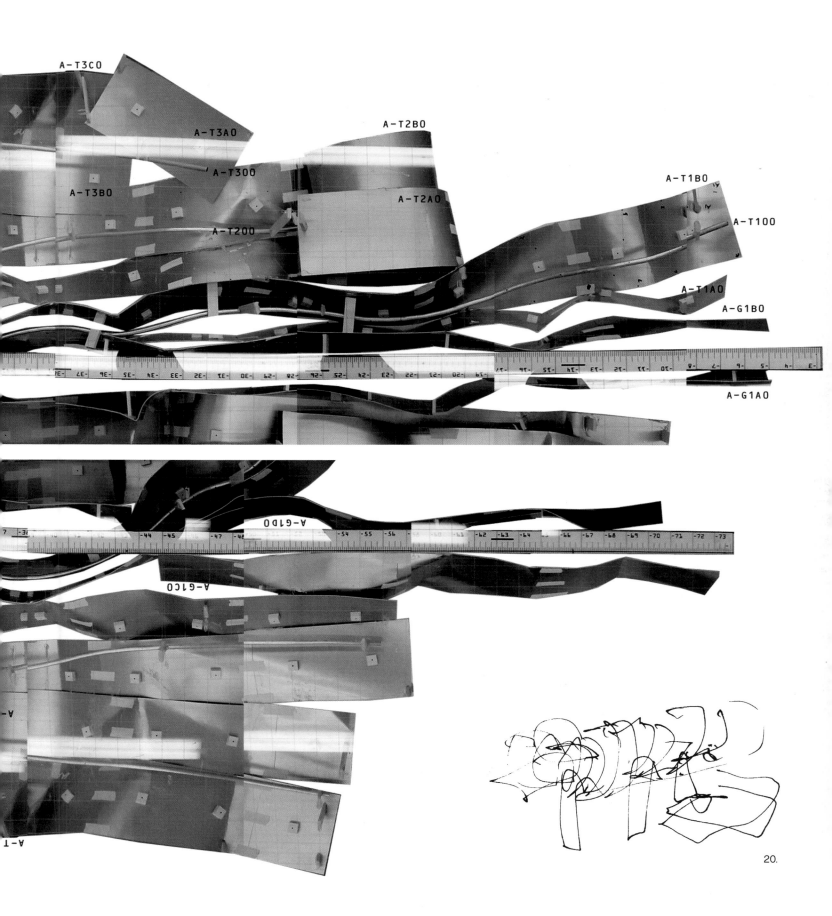

A-T3C0

A-T2B0

A-T3A0

A-T300

A-T1B0

A-T3B0

A-T2A0

A-T100

A-T200

A-T1A0

A-G1B0

A-G1A0

A-G1D0

A-G1C0

20.

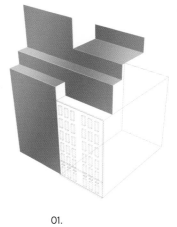

01.

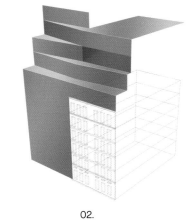

02.

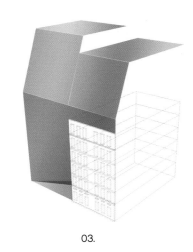

03.

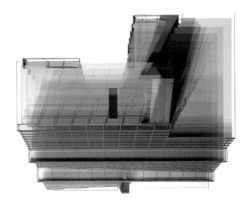

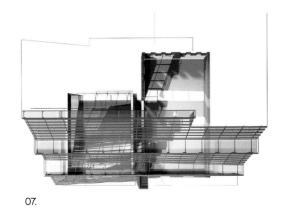

06.

07.

08.

09.

10.

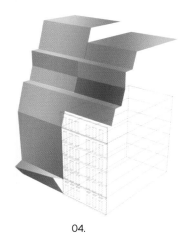

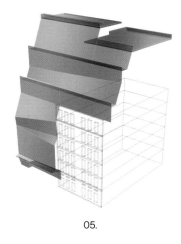

04.

05.

497 Greenwich Street

497 Greenwich Street
Archi-Tectonics
2004 Completion

This project transforms a derelict six-story warehouse and adjacent single-story garage into a 76,000-square-foot mixed-use facility with twenty-six residential lofts, as well as gallery and retail spaces.

The solution calls for the renovation of the existing structure, the addition of a four-story penthouse on top, and a new eleven-story residential building on the adjacent lot. The physical connections between the brick building and the glass-and-steel structure serve to mediate the project's binary elements—old and new, preservation and modernization, residential and commercial, public and private.

An undulating glass facade angles away from the street as it rises, reacting to local zoning and setback codes while providing residences with natural light and views of the nearby Hudson River to the west. Functionally,

the facade's materials contribute to the building's energy efficiency and sustainability.

A central core, containing vertical transportation, utilities, and other functions, offers multiple options for heating, cooling, and electronic connections in each of the units, as well as opportunities for expansion. The flexible internal structure accommodates personalized adaptation by individual occupants.

Six cantilevering balconies bridge the gap between the old and new structures. Terraces at higher levels span the width of the Greenwich Street elevation and create generous outdoor spaces.

The facade bends inward at the ground level to reveal the art gallery and retail spaces that contribute to the revitalization of this former industrial area, easing its transformation into an integrated residential neighborhood.

01. - 05. Greenwich Street facade: Inflection studies.

06. - 10. Building and curtainwall renderings. Building section looking south (fig. 09).

11.

12.

13.

14.

11. View to the south from eighth-floor terrace.

12. View looking up west elevation.

13. View looking north along Greenwich Street.

14. Interior view, sixth floor, looking west.

15. Greenwich Street elevation.

16. View looking down landscaped plaza behind the building.

15.

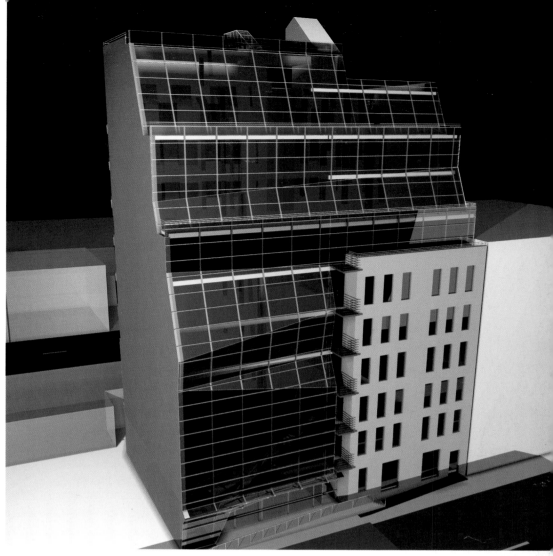

16.

Wooster Street Loft

Wooster Street
Archi-Tectonics
2001

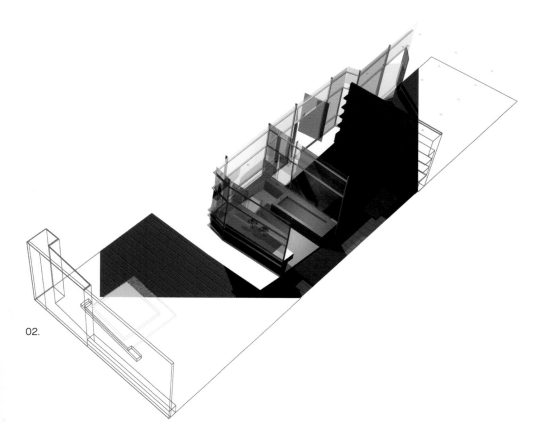

02.

This project adapts the fifth floor of a converted SoHo loft building to a 5,000-square-foot residence for an art collector. The design uses an undulating wall of translucent glass and aluminum to generate distinct zones— including public, private, and guest areas— while retaining a sense of continuity throughout the residence.

Instead of standard doors and enclosures, transitions into different spaces are accomplished through interlocking volumes that connect the rooms while maintaining visual privacy. Changing surface textures of walls and floors further delineate the spaces within the loft.

An open living room features large arched windows, which also provide light to the adjacent dining area. The kitchen, located within the fold of a wall section opposite the dining space, is flanked by a cantilevered

cement work surface that hovers over a pivoting breakfast bar made of translucent poured polyurethane.

Walls in the library and bedrooms are finished in walnut-veneered wood, with a matching customized desk and shelf unit in the library. A fireplace in the master bedroom stands apart from the main wall to form a semi-open hearth, allowing activity in the space beyond to be seen and heard through the fire. The bathroom, wrapped in glass planes, is designed as a free-floating unit with all functions sculpted into a single element.

The ceiling surface dips down to accommodate all mechanical, acoustical, and lighting equipment. An outdoor terrace is protected from the weather by a suspended structural glass roof that continues the folded planes of the ceiling within.

01. An undulating wall of glass and aluminum divides the loft into three program areas— private, public and guest.

02. Axonometric diagram of the library, the main bathroom and the master bedroom.

03.

04.

05.

06.

07.

01.

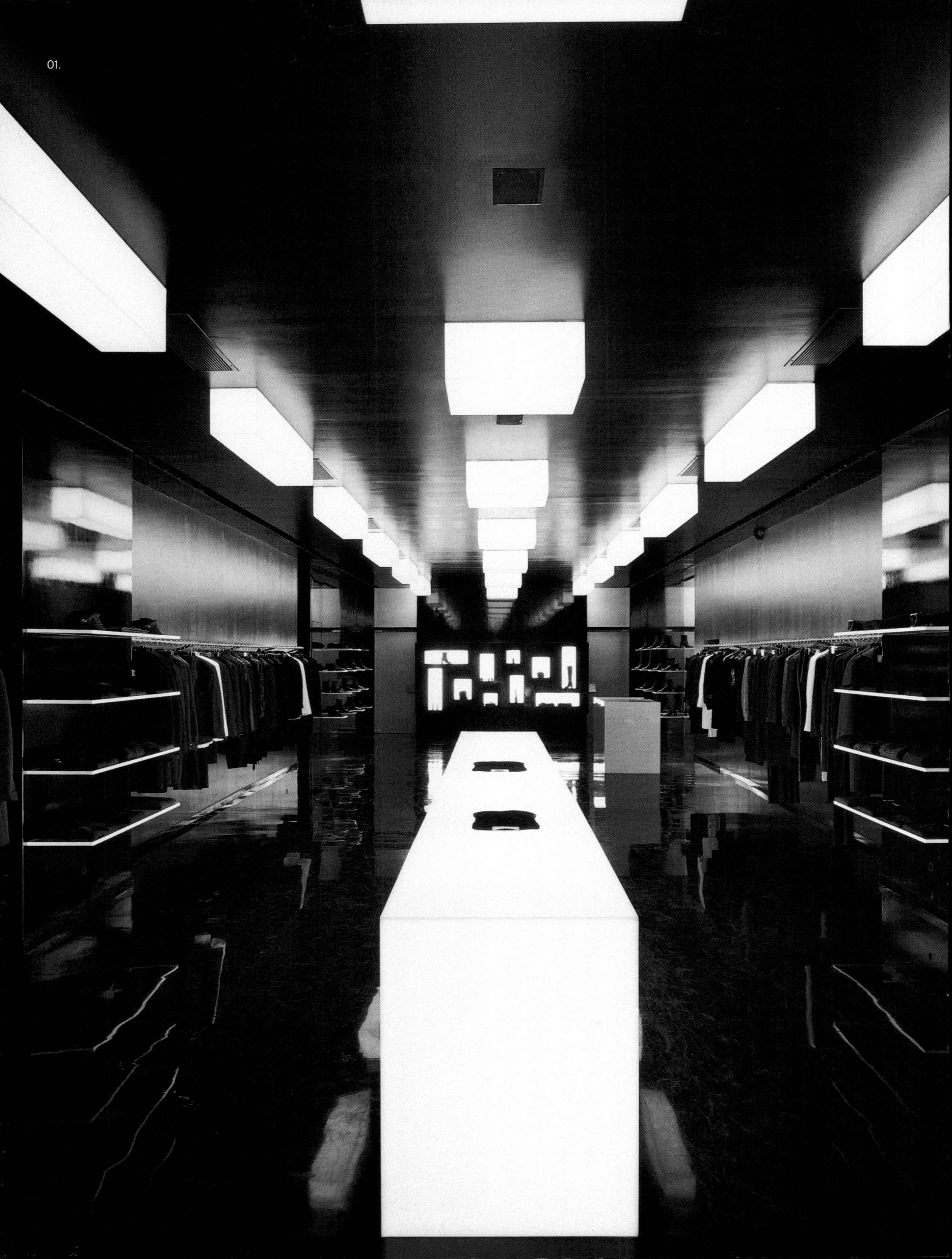

Costume National

108 Wooster Street
Sharples Holden Pasquarelli
1997

Ennio Capasa's minimalist designs for the Milan-based atelier Costume National inspired architects Sharples Holden Pasquarelli (SHoP) to use light and the absence of color to create a complimentary architecture. Behind a simple three-part storefront, the 2,500-square-foot retail program is contained within a rectangular space painted in gloss and matte black. Characterized as a black void, the combined effects of pigment and light dissolve the perception of ceiling and floor.

In the store's sea of black finishes, light becomes the dominant material. With the datum lines removed, the collection is organized by managing the intensity of light within the store. The ambient glow of the light boxes scattered throughout allows the enclosure to melt into darkness, while focused illumination showcases the highly articulated structure and materiality of the clothing itself. Cantilevered acrylic shelving lit with fiber optics float displays into the space. The overall effect is to create an ethereal environment for the merchandise.

01. Interior view looking north.

02. - 03. Entry sequence through Wooster Street
storefront.

04. Shelving strategies in accesories department.

01.

02.

03.

Issey Miyake Pleats Please

128 Wooster Street
Toshiko Mori Architect
1998

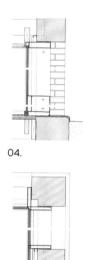

04.

05.

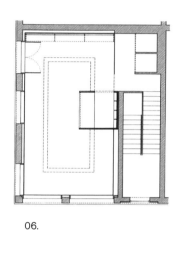

06.

The Pleats Please boutique in SoHo follows a brief similar to an uptown store Toshiko Mori previously designed for the house of Miyake in 1996, located on 77th Street and Madison Avenue. It required carving out a small retail program into the ground floor of a residential building within a designated historic district. The client suggested an urban presence for the new 1,000-square-foot store that addressed the specific character of the street. The existing building on the corner of Wooster and Prince Streets, while not landmarked, was erected as a tenement in 1852 and predates the cast-iron facades of its neighbors. The architect proposed a storefront that acts as an "infill" between the cast iron buildings, and accordingly developed a facade that preserves much of the brick and brownstone exterior. Glazing was recessed to create appropriate shadow lines consistent with surrounding buildings. The painted metal bulkhead at the foot of the plate glass was added externally as a contextual response.

The description of a showcase attains very literal properties once inside the store. To create what Mori refers to as an "internal facade," glass is transformed from a recessed external element into a delicate enclosure. Spanning floor to ceiling, the free-standing screen wraps around the corners to create a glass box that dematerializes the restricted space by manipulating levels of transparency, translucency and reflectivity inherent in the material.

The diffusion and refraction of light is controlled by the use of a film sandwiched between two panes of glass. The conceit creates variable levels of visibility through the glass as one navigates around the racks. Much like Miyake's approach to fabric in the invention of tactile effects, Mori exploits the materiality of glass as the principal medium in the transformation of the space, complimenting the product on display.

01. - 03. Interior views.

04. Wall section.

05. Corner section.

06. Floor plan.

07. Southeast corner, Wooster and Prince streets.

07.

01.

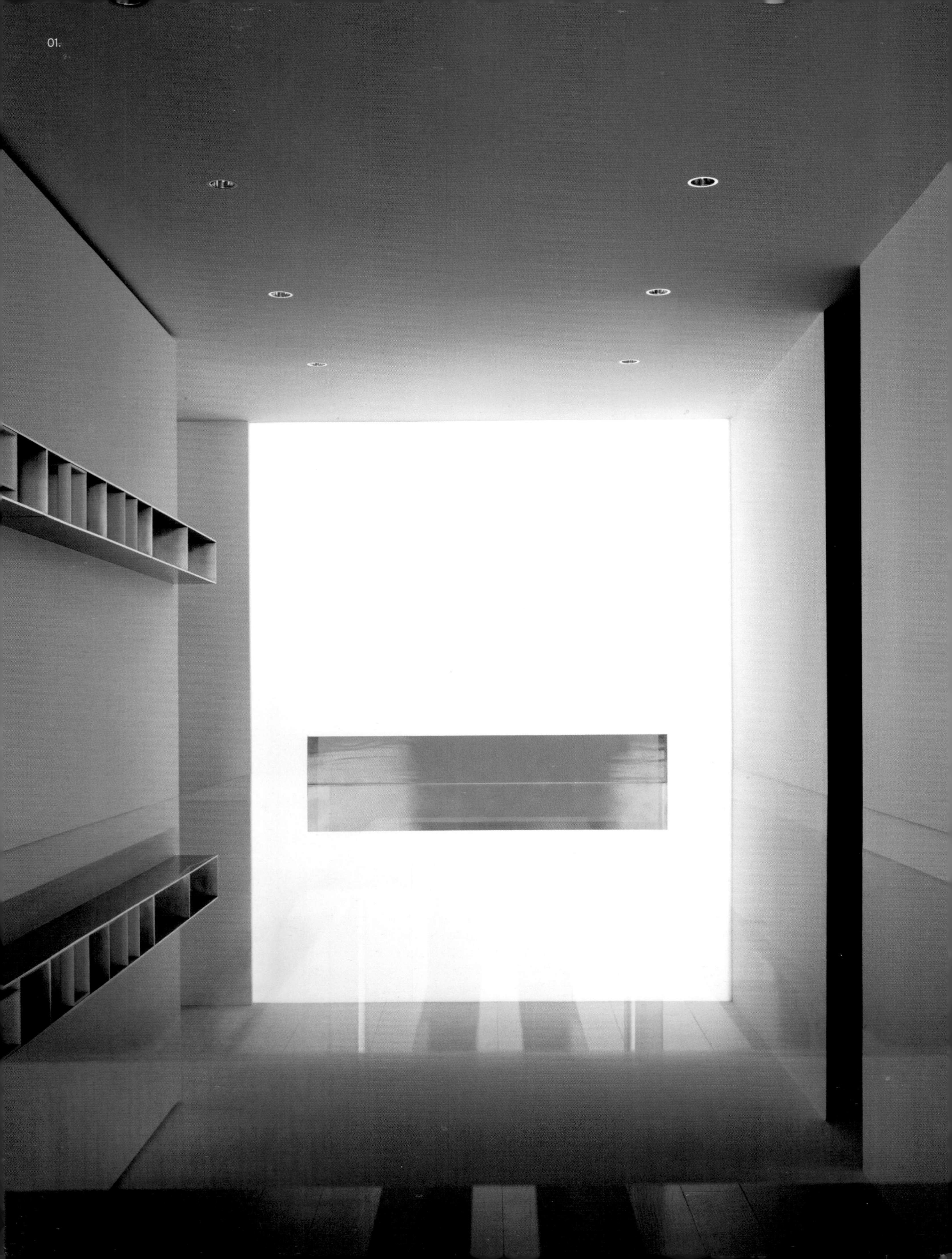

Mercer Street Loft

SoHo
Deborah Berke
2001

In 2001, the New York firm of Deborah Berke completed a 3,700 square-foot loft for Paris-born Fabien Baron, whose stint as art director under the late Elizabeth Tilberis at *Harper's Bazaar* ushered in an new era of elegance in American magazine design. Deborah Berke previously designed Baron's offices a decade ago and is certainly no stranger to her longtime client's orbit; in 1991, she was tapped to create Industria Superstudio, a cluster of cycloramas and event spaces on Washington Street that have become indispensable to New York fashion.

Intimating Baron's reductive layouts, the austere white interiors of the public and private spaces are interrupted by brief passages of color. The ubiquity of parallel lines within the space and a penchant for repeating—even standardizing—details mimic the printed page. Punctuating broad stretches of fine plaster, all the doors and windows are invariably floor-height. To break up the hermetic enclosure formed by the smooth walls and single-plate windows, the material palette accommodates a stained oak floor, oiled walnut accents, stainless-steel fixtures, a custom bathtub fashioned out of black schist and the client's collection of art objects. The loft is announced by a 1,200 square-foot living room and entry hall linking the program areas. The largest of the three bedrooms is separated from the hallway by a 15-foot wall of glass, the main dining room and study branch off the living room, and the kitchen is accessed through walnut doors.

01. View of the main hall from the dining room.

04.

05.

02. - 03. Living room views.

04. - 05. Views of the bathroom sink and bathtub, hewn out of black, Manhattan schist.

Prada New York Epicenter

575 Broadway
Office for Metropolitan Architecture
Architectural Research Office
2001

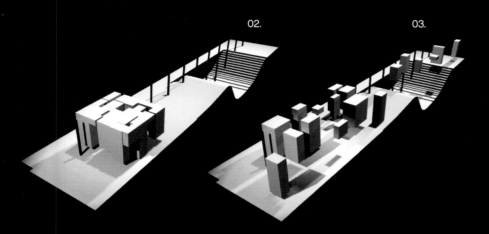

02.   03.

Armed with nearly two years' worth of research that cast shopping as a primary generative force in the transformation of contemporary cities, OMA set out to revamp the concept of the flagship store in downtown Manhattan. Instead of the simple enlargement of the typical Prada boutique (of which there are three uptown) Rem Koolhaas and Ole Scheeren opt for the creation of a full-fledged event—an 'epicenter' where "the commercial function is overlaid with a series of experiential and spatial typologies."

The Prada New York Epicenter is an interior conversion of the former Guggenheim Store in SoHo, on the corner of Broadway and Prince Street. The project's 23,000 square-feet are distributed between the ground floor and the basement of the building. To guide the customers to the retail areas in the cellar, the floor dips, and gradually rises back to street level.

Almost the width of the store, the stair made of zebra wood is used as an informal display space to try on shoes and browse through other accessories. With the push of a button, a stage folds out of the wave cresting towards

Broadway, turning the stair into an auditorium for performances, film projections, and lectures. Large metal cages for merchandise are suspended from an overhead track system and create singular shopping addresses, like inverted buildings in a street—a "hanging city." These display cases can contract at the back of the store into a solid volume, thereby freeing the space for public activities.

Located at the Broadway entrance, a round and fully glazed elevator displays accessories, enabling customers to shop while traveling vertically. It descends into a lounge located underneath the wave, where the main dressing rooms are visible, allowing for customers and passersby to engage in a participatory theater. The black-and-white marble floor is a reference to the first Prada store in Milan; its reflection gets distorted through the curved mirrored ceiling of the space. A translucent wall of polycarbonate covers the existing brick wall on the Prince Street side, and the application of wallpaper running the entire length promises an ever-changing environment. The north wall of the basement features a system of compact shelving that allows for the sequence and size of spaces to be altered according to

need. These Prada mint-green shelves contrast with the unfinished gypsum board walls and the wooden ceiling. With a separate entrance from Mercer Street, the all-white clinic area contains VIP rooms, tailors and catering facilities.

01. View of the storefront along Broadway.

02 - 03. Large wire cages for merchandise are suspended from an overhead rack system. Resembling a "hanging city," these display cases can contract into a box for stowage.

04. - 15. Sequence through the store, from first floor to basement. The store is conceived as specific insertions, both in relation to the immediate urban context, as well as the brand and its existing network of stores. The large zebrawood wave at the center of the store folds out to form a stage for events and performances at the push of a button (fig. 09).

05. 06.

09.

12.

13.

07.

08.

10.

11.

14.

15.

01.

02.

03.

Helmut Lang Parfumerie

81 Greene Street
Gluckman Mayner Architects
2001

This 3,100-square-foot SoHo retail space marks the launch of the Austriian atelier's fragrance line. Based on a modern interpretation of Old World apothecaries, the store provides a laboratory setting that supports the commercial aspects of selling perfume. The program includes a main retail space, a private consultation room, offices and laboratories. The store incorporates design elements from Lang's flagship store, designed by Gluckman Mayner in 1997, with modifications that accommodate the featured products.

Inside the narrow entryway, an installation by Jenny Holzer is part of an enameled steel wall that runs the length of the interior. A mirror image double stair descends along this wall, leading to research and development offices and laboratories. The vertical slice created by the wall and stair, combined with the installation's scrolling text, emphasize the length of the volume and draw the visitor inside. The main space is defined by three elements, all variations of concepts found in the flagship store. A full-height translucent glass wall, visible from the street, creates a backdrop to the product collection and lab displays. Opposite the installation wall is a product cabinet accented by a narrow, glass-lined slot that complements the products' glass bottles. A long, low cashier station, complete with touch-screen Internet access and white-glass countertop, occupies the body of the space, creating a stage for exchange between customer and consultant.

The intimate skylighted space behind the glass wall allows customers to receive private consultations. An amber glass window in the corner of this room extends the Parfumerie's space outside.

01. View of entry sequence featuring a permanent LED installation by Jenny Holzer.

02. View of main retail counter.

03. View of product cabinet.

Scholastic Building

557 Broadway
Aldo Rossi Studio di Archittetura
2001

Known unofficially as the Harry Potter building for the statue of J. K. Rowling's boy-wizard in the lobby, this SoHo building is the home of Scholastic Inc., one of the last independently owned—and certainly the most profitable—American publishers of books and educational materials for the youth market. Serving as the international headquarters for a company with wholly owned subsidiaries in four continents, the ten-story building occupies a coveted site on lower Broadway between Spring and Prince streets, with a secondary elevation on Mercer Street.

The Scholastic building is the only New York project by the late Milanese visionary Aldo Rossi. The prefabricated, cast-iron facades of SoHo had always intrigued the Pritzker Prize-winning architect and theorist, and it was not until the early 1990s that he secured a commission in the historic district. Assisted by protégé Morris Adjmi, Rossi executed the design with the zeal and reverence of a young practitioner armed with a newly minted degree. Rubbing shoulders with Ernest Flagg's precious Little Singer Building from 1903, the Scholastic building is an inspired exercise in contextualism. Drawing its cues from its steel and terra-cotta neighbor to the north and remembered details from the Hotel Il Palazzo (1987) in Fukuoka City, the principal elevation facing Broadway is composed of alternating bands of exposed green and red I beams. The horizontal movement created by these structural elements, which culminate in a red roof of three stacked girders, is visually opposed by the illusory vertical heft of precast columns fastened onto the steel frame. At the attic story, these four faux pillars split into seven smaller ones.

The project took a while to get off the ground, as the architects proposed a structure five floors higher than the five-floor limit imposed by the district's special zoning. Rossi's office and executive architects Gensler tendered design documents in 1995, and secured permission to build from the City Landmarks Preservation Commission only weeks before Rossi died in a car crash near Lake Maggiore on September 4, 1997. True to his mentor's original design, Morris Adjmi saw the project to completion in 2001.

01. View along Broadway, flanked by the Rouss and Little Singer buildings.

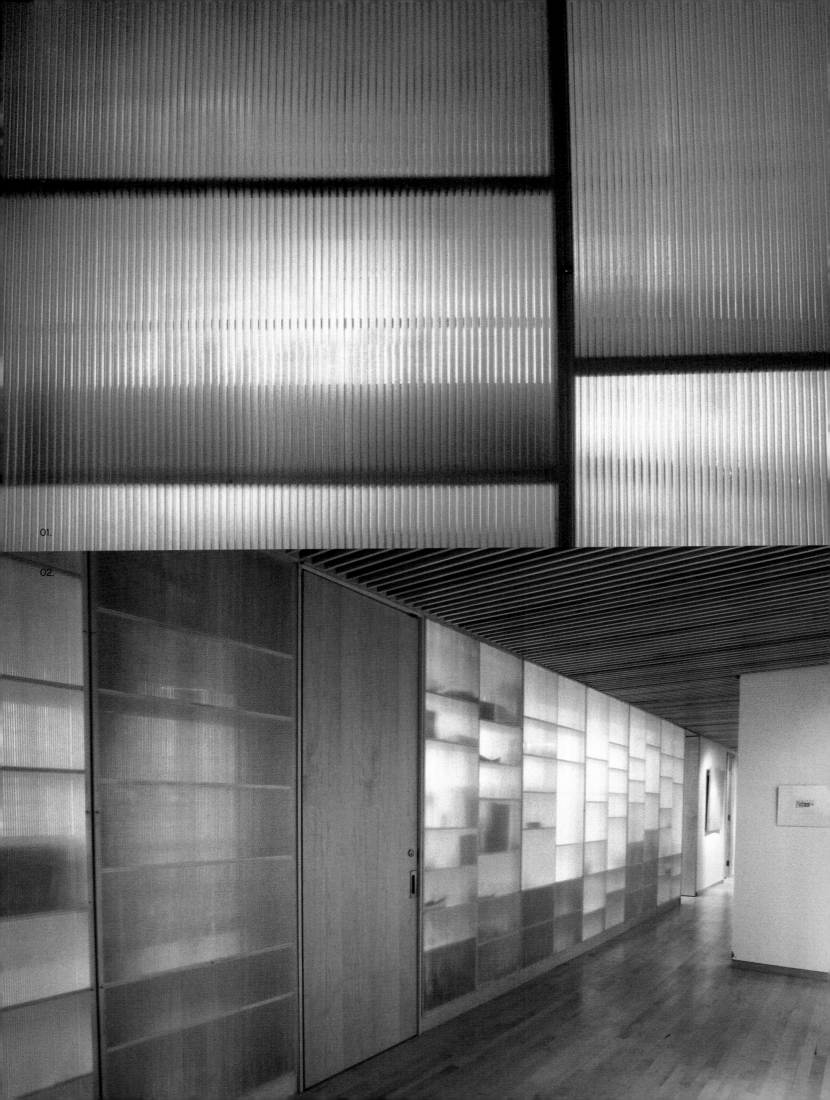

01.

02.

New York University
Asian / Pacific / American Studies

269 Mercer Street
Maya Lin Studio
David Hotson
1997

Occupying a floor within an academic and administrative building one block west of Broadway, the new Asian Pacific American Studies Department at New York University utilizes natural light throughout the space even though only two sides of the space benefit from direct sunlight.

Daylight is "shared" through the use of translucent walls along the perimeter offices and conference rooms that line the central gallery. This hallway, which would have otherwise been dark, is illuminated by light filtering through frosted panels that conceal the back shelves in the offices. The random arrangement of books creates a play of light and shadow, partially revealing the spaces beyond, yet preserving a sense of privacy in the offices. The striations that run the length of the textured panels regulate the light further, their vertical movement reflected in the wood-lath structure of the low ceiling.

Maya Lin conceived an inherently flexible office plan. Sliding panels hidden in the walls allow for a multiplicity of uses. The gallery opens up to the conference room, and this room in turn can divide into smaller rooms. The seminar room can be conjoined with the director's office, and private niches for study may similarly be merged with the larger program areas. Lending the place an intimate and contemplative character the aesthetic and operational strategies employed in the design reference—though not explicitly—details present in vernacular Asian and Polynesian architecture.

01. Detail of translucent panels.
02. View of the main gallery.

02.   03.

Byrd Hoffman Foundation

131 Varick Street
Stamberg Aferiat
1999

The Byrd Hoffman Foundation/RW Work Offices is the New York City headquarters of impresario and artist Robert Wilson. Established to raise funds for the client's Waterville Center workshops, the nonprofit foundation moved from its previous location to occupy 2,500 square-feet of a ninth-floor loft on Varick Street.

Exchanging ideas with Wilson—who is abroad for most of the year—mostly through fax, the New York partnership of Peter Stamberg and Paul Aferiat developed a light-filled working environment for the ten-person staff. Expanding themes that the client sought to preserve from the old office (and actually salvaging some elements from it), the architects reprised the use of translucent glass panels from the former office to demarcate the major program areas. Within the L-shaped plan are reception areas, a display archive and library, and six workstations. Set at partial-height, the twelve glass panes act like a continuous scrim, shielding the people and objects behind them without a commensurate reduction in available light to both work and reception spaces.

In combination, the sandblasted glass, white walls and ambient illumination produce a gallerylike space—an appropriate minimal backdrop for the client's own designs, which are strategically positioned throughout the space, including a number of sculptural furniture pieces from Wilson's own theatrical productions from the last two decades.

01. View of the library.

02. The reception area also features a display wall. A table and a flower sculpture by Robert Wilson are between two Carlo Mollino chairs.

03. The client designed the beech table in the reception area.

01.

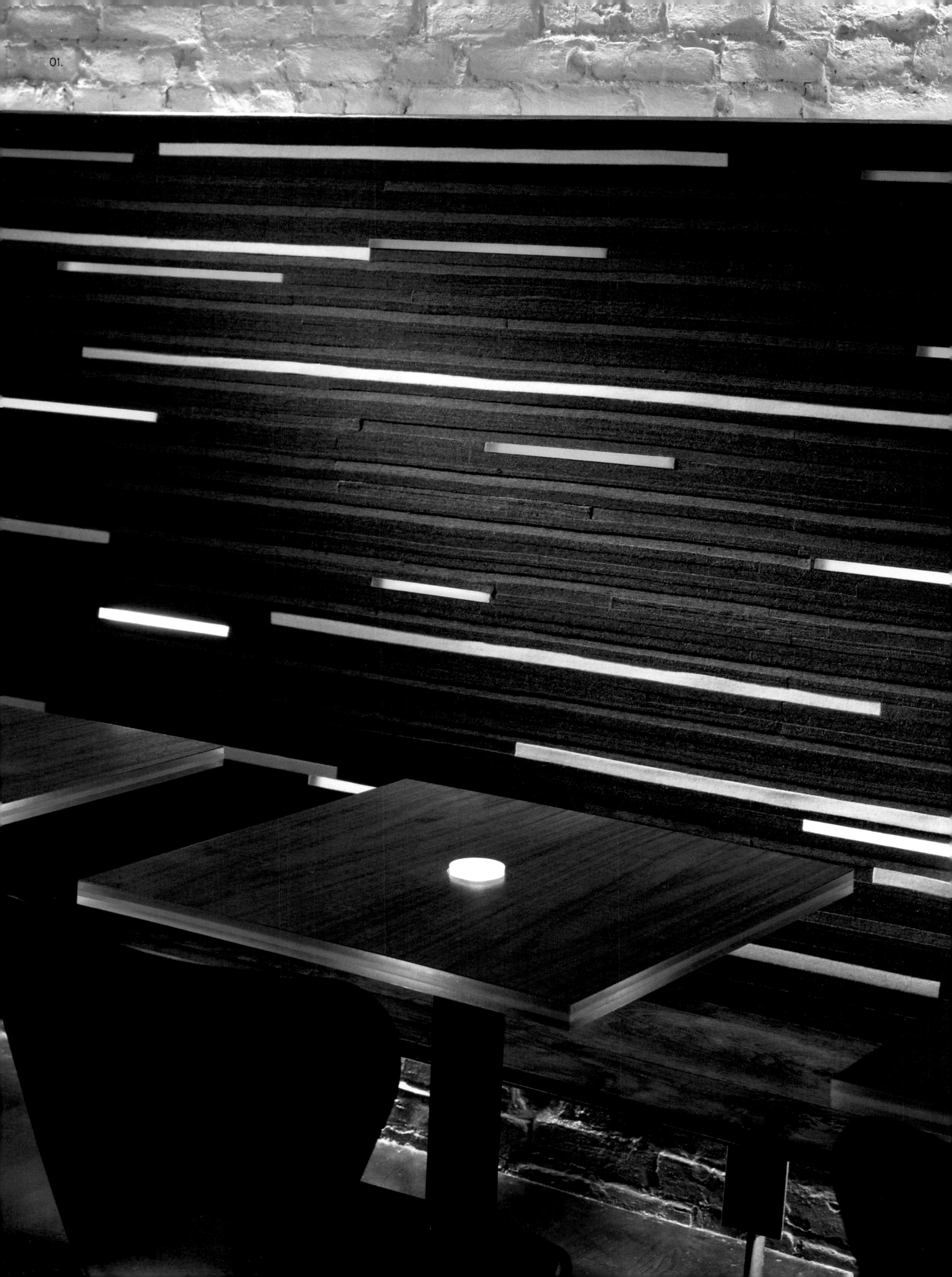

Lozoo

140 West Houston Street
Lewis Tsurumaki Lewis
2002

Inspired by the meals served at his grand-mother's table in Shanghai, silk-maker and accidental gourmand Greg Kan teamed up with Li Ping, the original proprietor of several long-running pan-Asian canteens in SoHo, to open Lozoo in the fall of 2002. The name approximates Chinese for green tea, and the highly imaginative cuisine itself might have more to do with Ping's provisional attitude to authenticity than Kan's memories, but the interior definitely has a tony, boom-time Shanghai feel to it. The downtown architects Lewis Tsurumaki Lewis make good on the Hudson-meets-the-Huangpu premise, devising an inventive solution to a series of site constraints.

Hemmed in by the narrow frontages that characterize this stretch of West Houston Street, the narrow entry sequence funnels into spacious yet intimate dining areas. The low ceiling in the front bar is addressed by supporting the bar from the basement, creating the sense that the floor of the entry room is suspended in a larger volume. This lower level, which accommodates support functions, is visible through an eight-inch gap in the floor of the bar.

A continuous datum divivides the walls into zones of dark and light at eye level, and unifies the five distinct spaces—bar, intermediate dining room, main dining room, outdoor garden, and bathroom—of the existing configuration. Mirrored on the opposing walls by a stained wood skirt, a continuous banquette lined with industrial felt wraps from the entry room into the main dining room, providing sound absorption and visually unifying the rooms. These layers of dark felt—distressed by random light strips—emphasize horizontal movement through the restaurant, and are offset by a corrugated vertical effect in the main dining area.

01. View of the bar area. Lozoo incorporates four distinct dining areas.

02. Detail: Along the banquette, thick layers of felt are punctuated by horizontal light strips.

03. Datum diagram: The walls are divided into zones of dark and light at eye level.

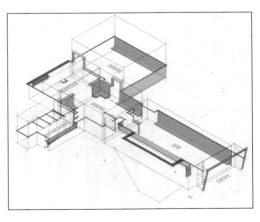

03.

04.

04. View looking into the main dining area in the back. Horizontal layers of dark felt contrast with a vertical effect inset with recessed lamps.

05. Natural light enters the main dining area through a large skylight.

06. The garden is open for dining in the summer.

07. View of the unisex bathroom.

05.

06.

07.

01.

Morton Loft

Greenwich Village
Lot/ek
1997

02.

Naples-born Ada Tolla and Giuseppe Lignano of Lot/ek (pronounced "low-tech") were retained by an IT consultant to design a residence in the West Village during the heady days of the high-tech boom. The brief seemed simple enough: to renovate a loft on the fourth floor of a former parking garage. The architects responded with typical wit and aplomb, suggesting that a 40-foot petroleum tank—separated from its trailer bed—form the nucleus of the new space. Cut in half, the shells were hoisted up by crane, and inserted into the bare 645-foot loft through a window.

No other walls or partitions were erected. The aluminum shells themselves were to enclose intimate spaces within. One half was laid on its side along the short axis of the room. Bolted at both ends to the structural walls, the twenty-foot drum was positioned close to the ceiling to accommodate two sleeping pods, their interiors painted a deep yellow. Two hatchback doors were cut on the side facing the large window. The other half of the tank was stood on its end to form two bathrooms, one placed on top of the other. To access the bunks and the second bathroom, a network of catwalks was installed, with a ladder descending to earth.

The use of "objects that already have a life" is integral to the improvisational character of the Lot/ek way of architecture. In adaptively reusing petroleum tanks (and in other cases, discarded truckbeds, refrigerators and shipping containers), their projects reference a philosophical precedent that has more to do with "found" art objects than it does any conception of environmental sensitivity. Which isn't to say that the architects pay only scant attention to issues of sustainability: their idiosyncratic worldview just happens to practically—if unintentionally—address those as well.

03.

04.

05.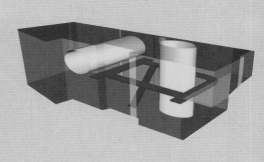

06.

03. - 05. The tanks were hoisted in place by a crane and inserted into the loft through the window. One half was stood on its end to provide bathrooms on the upper and lower levels.

06. - 07. Views of the sleeping tank over the dining table with the doors open and closed.

Perry Street Towers

173 and 176 Perry Street
Richard Meier & Partners
2003 Completion

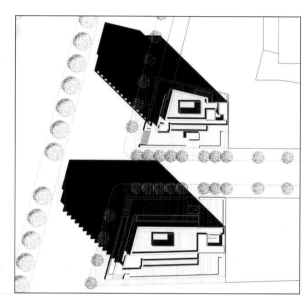

02.

Standing on the north and south corners of Perry and West Street, these two residential towers are Richard Meier's first built projects in Manhattan since the renovation of the massive Westbeth Artists' Housing Co-op on 463 West Street in 1969.

The prominent waterfront siting and the low, surrounding neighborhood confer on the sixteen-story Perry Street buildings a dispro-portionate impact on this stretch of the Hudson River skyline. Lean and transparent, the towers are both sheathed in a curtainwall system of laminated glass and white metal panels, and detailed with vestigial sunshades that run the height of the Hudson River elevations. Each floor houses one individual apartment of approximately 1,800 square-feet in 173 Perry Street (the north tower); and 3,750 square-feet in 176 Perry Street (the south tower). The individual apartments are

bathed in natural light, and offer panoramas of lower Manhattan, the Hudson River and the New Jersey riverfront. To maximize views, the cores are set against the narrow east facades. Large operable windows are arranged in a modulated pattern with perimeter radiant heating, accommodating floor-to-ceiling glass walls on the apartment floors. Clad in translucent green panes, all-glass balconies project out from the north and south-facing exposures.

Both buildings are entered from Perry Street. The tower at 176 Perry Street is planned with a cafe at ground level, accessible from West Street. This amenity overlooks a reflecting pool that will be open to the neighborhood. The buildings form a gateway into Hudson River Park, a network of green and paved spaces stretching from Battery Park City to 59th Street.

01. View to south, along West Street.

02. Site plan.

03.

03. View along West Street waterfront park.

04. - 07. Views of the north tower on 173 Perry Street

04.

05.

06.

07.

01.

02.

03.

04.

Vitra New York

29 Ninth Avenue
ROY
2002

05.

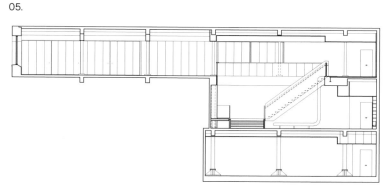

06.

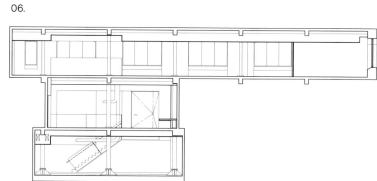

Vacating a third-floor perch on 21st Street and Fifth Avenue, the New York City operation of the Swiss furniture manufacturer Vitra moved southwest to a three-story facility within the Meatpacking District in late 2002. Renovating an existing commercial building on the west side of Ninth Avenue between 13th and 14th streets, Lindy Roy reworked a simple layout to integrate 13,000 square-feet of program into a true showcase for the client's unrivalled catalog of twentieth-century chairs.

Panes of vision glass span the width of the storefront, bisected by an illuminated rectangular wall displaying the company's graphic identity. Behind the glass, a triple-height vertical shaft permits natural light to penetrate throughout the interior. Created by removing parts of the existing concrete slabs, this space is one of two atrium-like openings that operationally link three allied programs: a gallery in the cellar, retail store at street level, and the main showroom functions on the enlarged second floor.

Sheathed in rubber, grey "tongues" curl out to form display ledges from the second-floor loft to the levels below. Lapping into the atria from the floorplates above, these animated forms visually unite the three floors as they

add a sculptural flourish to the minimal idiom employed throughout the interior shell.

A platform bridging the atrium opening at the ground floor leads to an elevated first-floor retail area. A staircase just inside the entrance descends to the basement-level exhibition space.

07.

01. View from second level of rubber-coated display "tongue" and concrete stair leading down to basement gallery.

02. Second floor showroom.

03. View from basement gallery of "tongue" and the underside of the concrete stair bridging street entrance with retail level.

04. View of the Ninth Avenue entrance from the retail level.

05. Section looking north.

06. Section looking south.

07. Ninth Avenue storefront with signage by 2x4.

08. View from second level of walnut stair, with stainless treads leading to a furniture display shelf backed by an illuminated polycarbonate wall.

09. View of second level showroom.

10. The wall-mounted porthole displays for Vitra's miniature modern chairs.

11. View from entrance of concrete stair bridging sidewalk with retail level, walnut furniture display shelf, and illuminated polycarbonate wall.

12. View of retail level "tongue," walnut shelf and stair leading to second level.

10.

11.

12.

01.

02.

03.

04.

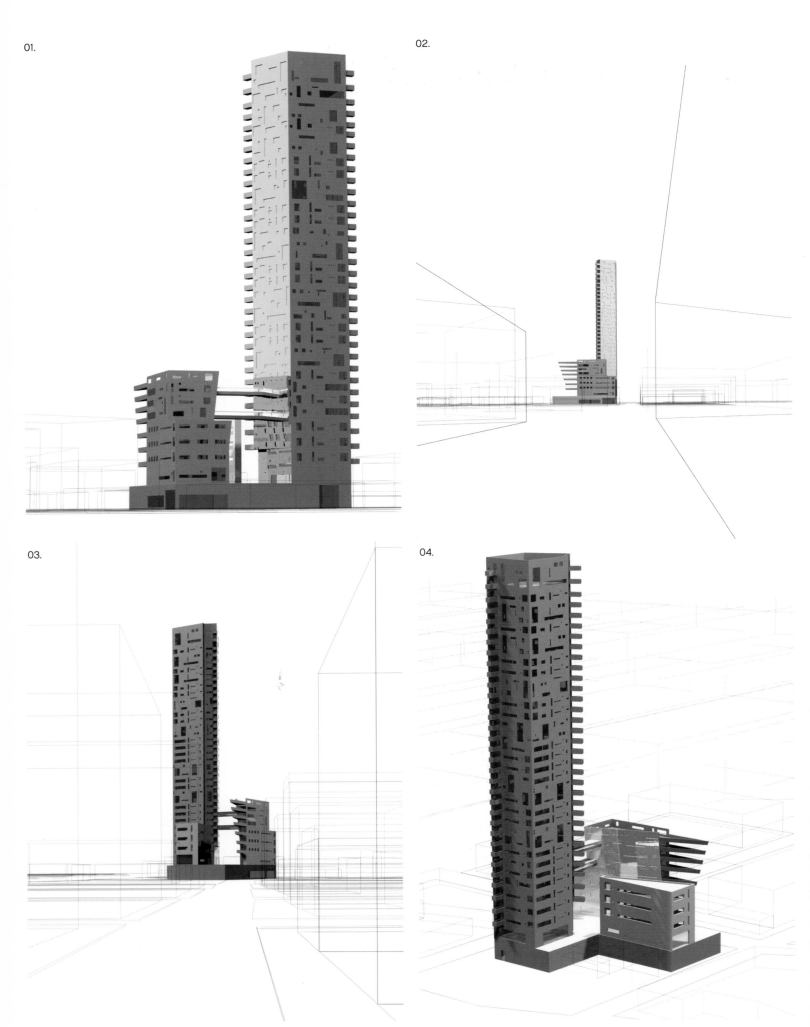

Gansevoort Market Tower

848 Washington Street
Architectures Jean Nouvel
Design Completed 2001

05.

This development is planned for a triangular waterfront site on Washington and Little West 12th Streets, bordered to the north by 13th Street. Pending approval, it will stand as one of the tallest structures along the Hudson River north of Canal Street. Architectures Jean Nouvel conceived the tower as a 32-story condominium in 2001, but the developer has since reprogrammed it into a 200-room hotel to avoid the residential and parking variances required by a neighborhood famously zoned for light manufacturing and commercial use. In tandem with the rezoning issues brought about by the original residential configuration, some community groups still object to the tower's projected height of nearly 500 feet.

Occupying a trapezoidal footprint, the tower assumes a slender, distinctive form, something the architect likens to an industrial chimney. Rendered primarily in glass and steel, the surface is etched with large and small cut-out windows, their random placement contrasting with ordered rows of balconies running the length of two opposing elevations. The development straddles the terminus of the Highline, an elevated freight track running from just south of Gansevoort Street to Eleventh Avenue and 34th Street. With plans to convert the derelict two-track railway into a 20,000-square-foot park, two smaller structures an eight-story and a five-story wedge are planned at the foot of the tower on either side of the historic viaduct. Both buildings are intended for commercial use; the taller of the two connects to the skyscraper via covered catwalks.

The project will be the fourth hotel planned in and around the dwindling Meatpacking District—and the soon-to-be-designated Gansevoort Market Historic District. It was preceded by the new Hotel Gansevoort on 13th Street and Ninth Avenue, the SoHo House on 13th and Hudson, and the Maritime Hotel inside the portholed envelope of the former Covenant House (and originally the National Maritime Union Building) on 16th and Ninth.

01. View from the northeast.
02. View from the east.
03. View from the southwest.
04. View from the south.
05. West elevation, view from New Jersey.

01.

02.

03.

04.

05.

06.

07.

Chelsea Carwash

15th Street and 10th Avenue
Cybul and Cybul
Christopher Grabé
Base
2000

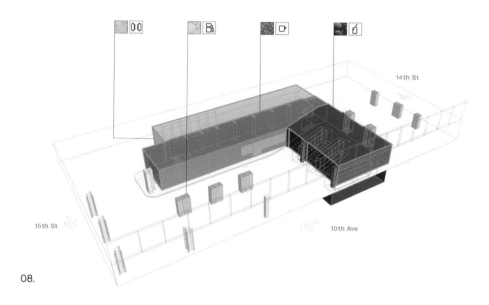

08.

The design and construction of Chelsea Carwash proved to be an extremely complex undertaking for a building of its type. This full-service carwash, deli and gas and lube station is located underneath the tracks of the Highline, on 15th Street and 10th Avenue. Community interest in protecting the abandoned freight railroad, and its proposed conversion into a pedestrian corridor connecting Greenwich Village to Chelsea and west midtown, imposed a number of design and engineering challenges, the most crucial being the preservation of the stretch of rail directly above the mixed-use facility.

The design team, led by the Edgewater, New Jersey, practice of David and Martin Cybul consulted with CSX, the owner of the old freight line to develop a comprehensive report on existing conditions. The findings required the restoration of the trestles abutting the site, and the encroaching Hudson River water table required the fabrication of a large reinforced bathtub to protect the gasoline tanks.

The design solution emphasizes the industrial mass of the Highline by contrasting its steel structure with a wall of glass, devised by Christopher Grabé. Composed of rectangular window panels tacked onto a light frame of steel tubes, the facade is stretched along the width of the block facing the West Side Highway. The steel supports of the railroad brace the transparent enclosure on one side. Extended well above the tracks, the lattice of glass and steel acts like a massive billboard, announcing its program to oncoming traffic with an environmental signage program developed by the design firm Base, headquartered in London and Brussels.

The interior spaces underscore the concept of movement and transparency as glass partitions allow visual access to much of the automotive facility. Replicating patterns along the main elevation, the garage doors and glass walls of the lube station even offer glimpses of the mechanical guts below grade.

01. - 03. Braced by the Highline, the steel-and-glass facade reveal the functions of the facility

04. - 07. Sequence through carwash, gas and lube station.

08. Axonometric plan.

09. The tip box.

09.

Lot 61

550 West 21st Street
Diane and Rafael Viñoly
1998

Bungalow 8

515 West 27th Street
2001

Hewn out of an abandoned truck garage on 21st Street and Eleventh Avenue, Rafael and Diane Viñoly's very first New York *boîte*—for nightclub entrepreneur Amy Sacco—debuted in the summer of 1998. Though much of the exterior shell was left untouched, few reminders of the building's humble industrial origins remain beyond the double-height ceilings of the 5,500-square-foot bar and restaurant. Much of everything else carted into the space instead bears evidence of west Chelsea's transition from a post-manufacturing littoral to the unrivaled pole of contemporary art in North America.

Strewn with multicolored cast-rubber seating Mrs. Viñoly allegedly salvaged from a mental institution, the architect pair put a premium on plush and flexibility to create a modish retreat with its very own fireplace and walk-in wine cellar (but a rather thoughtless attempt by the owner to introduce a disco ball was dismissed out of hand). Behind the contoured mass of the two-ton zinc bar, transparent sliding screens on I-beam rails can split the plan into discrete rooms, permitting Lot 61 to host private fetes while other sections of the lounge remain open.

Artifacts of the neighborhood trade are tacked high on the walls. One of Damien

Hirst's "Spot" paintings, *3-(5-chloro-2-Hydro-exphenylazo)-4,5-Dikydroxy-2,7-Napthea-leneisulfonic* (1998), and Jim Lander's *Chachi* (1998) hover over the north and south banquettes; Jim Hodges' neon doodles greet nighthawks in the bathroom stalls. A David Salle originally presided over the semi-secluded main dining room.

But Manhattan nightspots tend to emit the most ephemeral of lights, and Lot 61 burned its brightest a few years back. To make up for some of the lost luster, Sacco and the Viñolys launched a new bar in 2001, half the size of their previous collaboration and a short jaunt from 21st Street. Behind a facade of rusty corrugated roofing, Bungalow 8 is practically invisible apart from a telling "No Vacancy" sign. It is ostensibly an exclusive haunt—and a very minor urban legend has grown out of access keys handed out Gramercy Park–style by its proprietress. Upon entry, the chief architectural feature of the tropical-themed space is a huge skylight. Supported by a steel frame painted a taxicab yellow, the opening irradiates its daytime customers with light filtered through a copse of live palms, its fronds casting real shadows on a wall-length photographic mural of busy swimming pools by artist Lucas Michael.

01. View of dining area with Sean Lander's *Chachi* (1998) in background.

02. View of entry on north side of 21st Street.

03. The two-ton zinc bar.

03.

04.

04. Lot 61: A painting by David Salle overlooks the semi-secluded dining room.

05. Bungalow 8: View of wall-sized mural by
Lucas Michael.

06. Bungalow 8: Exterior view of corrugated tin
facade on 27th Street.

01.

02.

Eyebeam Atelier

West 21st Street
Diller + Scofidio
Design Completed 2001

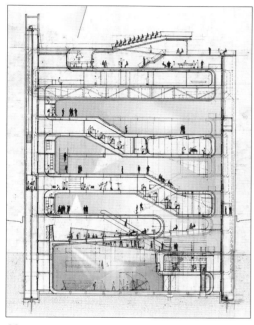

03.

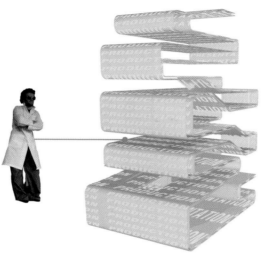

04.

Elizabeth Diller and Ricardo Scofidio's scheme for the Eyebeam Atelier/Museum of Art and Technology is the winning entry in an invited competition between twelve firms. Intended for a mid-block site between Tenth and Eleventh Avenues and adjacent to the Paula Cooper Gallery in Chelsea, the brief for the 90,000-square-foot museum required the merger of four discrete uses: gallery, theater, school and production facility.

In response to this programmatic challenge, the design solution was derived from a simple concept: a flexible ribbon that situates *production* (atelier) on one side, and *presentation* (museum/theater) on the other. Developed with the engineering consultancy Arup, this concrete ribbon alights from the street and rises to the full height of the building like a giant sidewinder.

In section, floors curve up to form walls, transition into ceilings, and slip back into floors as the ribbon ascends. As it snakes from left to right, this infinite loop alternately encircles production or presentation areas. The hybrid program also draws together two diverse communities: the building's residents (students, artists and staff) and its visitors (museum and theatergoers). The melding of functions compels each user group to enter the space of the other as they move up and down the building. As described by the architects, this series of interrelationships achieves greater complexity "when a loop of ribbon at one level is sheared in half and slipped into alignment with a level above or below." This constant realignment of planes creates its own internal drama, a "controlled contamination [that] juxtaposes technical processes with their effects, contrasting people at work with people at leisure."

01. 21st Street elevation: View looking east.

02. Building entry.

03. Section looking south.

04. The museum is conceived as a pliable ribbon that locates production to one side, and presentation on the other.

05. View to west. To the left is the two-story Paula Cooper Gallery, Gluckman Mayner Architects (1999).

06. Shared computer lab and classroom.

07. View of mediatheque.

08. View of theater.

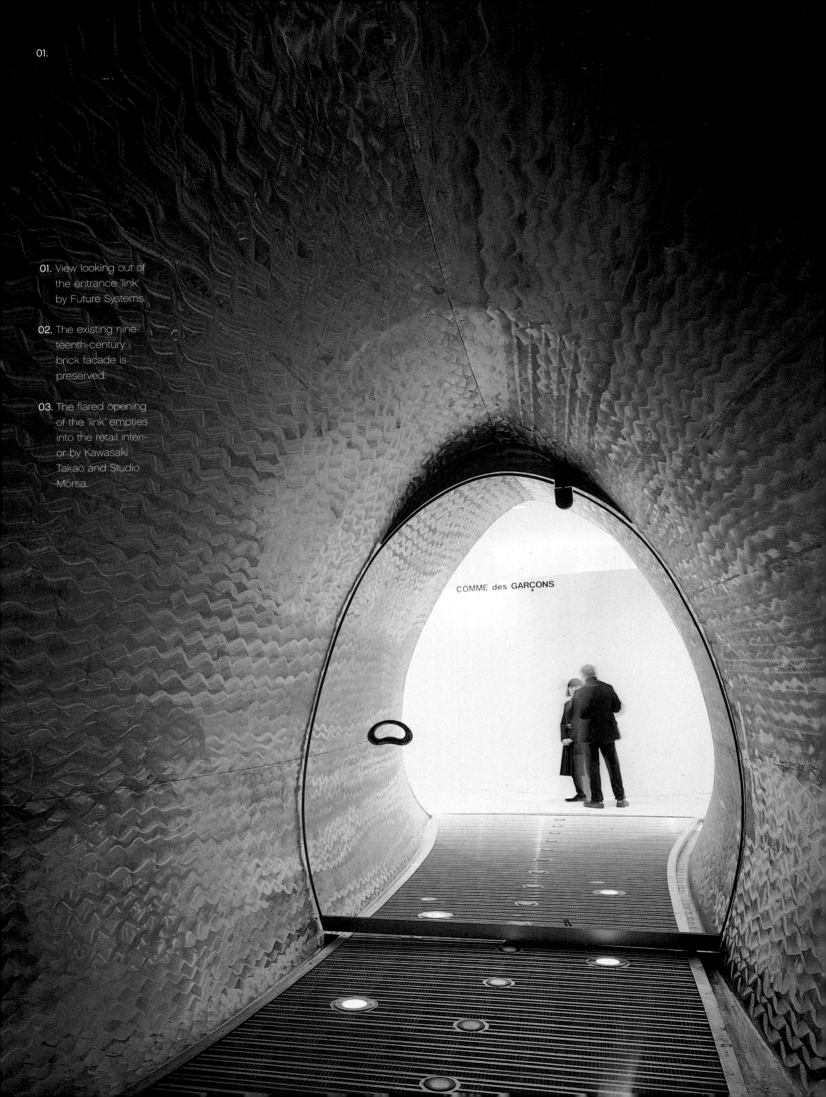

01.

01. View looking out of the entrance 'link' by Future Systems.

02. The existing nineteenth-century brick facade is preserved.

03. The flared opening of the 'link' empties into the retail interior by Kawasaki Takao and Studio Morsa.

COMME des GARÇONS

Comme des Garçons

555 West 22nd Street
Future Systems
Takao Kawasaki
Studio Morsa
1999

On the heels of art galleries emigrating from SoHo, Comme des Garçons moved its Wooster Street operation to Chelsea in 1999. Inserted into a row of warehouses mid-block from Richard Gluckman's DIA Center for the Arts (1987) on Eleventh Avenue, the new store preserves the existing brick facade, as well as old trade signage and external wrought-iron fire escapes.

An asymmetric aluminum tube—designed by the London-based firm Future Systems—is grafted behind a brick entrance arch.

Dubbed the "link," the structure provides gallery hoppers a dramatic transition from the street into the spare, luminous interior of the store. Lit by a single row of marker lights, the walls of the 20-foot serpentine link compact at midpoint, and flare into openings at either end. The skin of the tube was machine-fabricated, its parts welded in situ, then abraded by hand with an industrial-grade sander.

Not entirely inside or outside, the tunnel formally negotiates between the nineteenth-

century exterior and the contemporary retail environment designed by Takao Kawasaki—a long-time architectural collaborator of Comme des Garçons designer Rei Kawakubo—and Studio Morsa. Painted a cool white, the store walls contort, shear and fragment into abstract forms, dividing the shopping area into small stages well suited for a collection that is by turns minimal and baroque.

501 West 23rd Street

501 West 23rd Street
Smith and Thompson Architects
1997

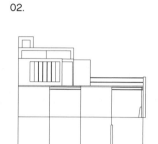
02.

03.

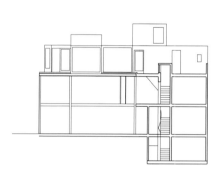
04.

05.

A pioneer building in the development of the Chelsea arts district in the latter half of the 1990s, this three-story art gallery is located on a busy corner formed by Tenth Avenue and 23rd Street. At the fringes of a residential neighborhood dotted with gas stations, light manufacturing lofts, bars, and restaurants, the structure is a few feet from the elevated tracks of the disused Highline. The heavy steel plates that clad the southern and eastern exposures—their use informed partly by the rusting train trestles—shield the interior elements of the program. Absorbing the noise from the street, these 10-by-10-foot and 10-by-20-foot sheets are tacked onto iron

girders and are arranged to form wide gaps, or else variously notched to give its users views of the city beyond. The panels, sealed with a paraffin-based coating, form a steel hedge around a two-story sculpture garden paved with white pebbles.

Accessed through the garden, the first two floors are dedicated exhibition spaces enclosed within a glass box, its mullions and other exterior details painted white. The top floor is actually an architectural studio, and its furnishings can be easily disassembled and set aside to accommodate events held in concert with the tenant galleries.

01. East elevation, along Tenth Avenue.

02. South elevation.

03. Section looking north.

04. Section looking west.

05. East elevation.

06. Ground floor plan.

06.

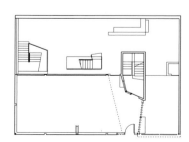

07.

08.

09.

10.

12.

07. - 08. Third floor, architects' offices.

09. - 10. Entry-level gallery.

11. Sculpture garden.

12. Southwest corner, 23rd Street and 10th Avenue.

01.

02.

03.

Mary Boone Gallery

541 West 24th Street
Gluckman Mayner Architects
2000

Completed in 2000, this 3,700-square-foot renovation of an existing brick warehouse in Chelsea complements the client's uptown gallery, also designed by Gluckman Mayner, in 1995. This design derives its layout, materials and details from the earlier Mary Boone Gallery at 745 Fifth Avenue, while manipulating these elements to accommodate existing conditions in the new space. Modern finishes and materials are juxtaposed against the historic detailing of the wood trusses and planks that remain exposed in the ceiling of the exhibition space.

The design uses the original wood structure to organize the building's plan, with the bays of the bow trusses driving the layout of the spaces. Thirteen-foot plaster ceilings in the ancillary reception, office and showroom areas accentuate the dramatic volume of the gallery.

Each of the three main rooms receives natural light in a different way. A 12-foot-wide translucent skylight runs above the length of the 24-foot-high display wall, creating excellent lighting conditions for viewing art. A small central skylight provides natural light to the back room, while the floor-to-ceiling translucent glass storefront illuminates the reception area.

The floor is a steel-troweled concrete slab, made lighter through the use of white Portland cement. Lightly tinted artisan plaster walls and ceilings form the gallery spaces. The limited palette of materials includes solid aluminum plate shelves, brushed aluminum laminate cabinetry, translucent glass and plastic, and the exposed wood of the original structure.

01. View of 24th Street facade.

02. Principal exhibition space with view of the skylight and exposed roof trusses.

03. Reception and office.

01.

02.

03.

Gagosian Gallery

555 West 24th Street
Gluckman Mayner Architects
2000

Located in Chelsea, this 25,000-square-foot space—formerly a garage dating to the 1940s—combines the scale of a small museum with the flexibility to accommodate a variety of exhibition requirements. The architects achieved height clearance for large-scale sculpture installations by raising the roof structure over the 6,000-square-foot primary gallery space, and by replacing two existing steel trusses with new, shallower trusses. The resulting raised roof provides column-free, long-term installation gallery space with the capacity to house large-scale sculptures.

The program includes a 2,400-square-foot main gallery, along with two smaller skylit galleries that total 3,600 square-feet. A private stock showroom features 23-foot-high viewing walls for displaying paintings from the adjacent stock racks, while a smaller special-purpose gallery opens to the sidewalk for site-specific installations. The remainder of the program space consists of a small prints and video showroom, storage space, and office and support spaces with additional private and semi-private showrooms.

The exterior facade is constructed of brick and precast concrete, with anodized aluminum and sandblasted glass storefront materials. A ten-foot-high polycarbonate clerestory window, which wraps around the building, bathes the interior space in natural light during the day and allows the interior lighting at night to serve as a beacon visible from the West Side Highway.

01. View of the northeast corner of 24th Street and Eleventh Avenue. An installation of Richard Serra's *Torqued Ellipses* (1997) is visible through the open "garage doors."

02. Interior view showing clerestory and roof truss.

03. Main entrance on 24th Street side.

01.- 02. Views of the
exhibition spaces
with installations by
Jenny Holzer and
Louise Bourgeois.

03. View of 27th Street
facade.

01.

02.

03.

Cheim & Read Gallery

558 West 27th Street
Gluckman Mayner Architects
1999

The brief for this project required the conversion of a 6,000-square-foot taxi garage into three separate galleries, two showrooms, administrative offices and storage spaces for Cheim & Read, which moved from its previous location on West 23rd Street.

The new gallery features a cast-in-place concrete facade—created by a technique commonly used for pouring building foundations with oversized glass panel doors. Upon entering, visitors come to a dome-vaulted gallery with a 25-foot ceiling that terminates at a square oculus. Five flared and baffled skylights provide natural lighting throughout the building, affording unobstructed views of the art by concealing the light fixtures.

Windows in the reception area feature anodized aluminum and gray tinted heat-strengthened glass. The interior spaces utilize white Portland cement floors, while incorporating the existing brick walls, timber roof, and steel and cast-iron columns.

Materials used in the administrative area include translucent laminate and custom stainless-steel cabinetry. An operable 400-square-foot clerestory window provides natural light and ventilation to this area. Complementing this window is a skylight that illuminates the floor-to-ceiling library.

01.

Glass

287 Tenth Avenue
Thomas Leeser
2001

02.

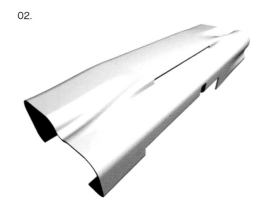

Flanked by the automotive glass shop that contributed to its name, this lounge is one of a triad of nightspots German-born Thomas Leeser designed in 2001, along with the Nolita wine bar :bot on Mott Street and the late, lamented Williamsburg restaurant Pod, which briefly burned on North Seventh Street between Bedford Avenue and Berry Street. Having previously designed the seminal Chelsea trattoria Bottino (1998) on 26th Street and the Klemens Gasser and Tanja Grunert Gallery (2000) on 19th Street, Leeser returned to the art district, financed by restaurateur Danny Emerman—the perpetrator of the erstwhile 1980s art world hangout Borocco— who was also the client at Bottino and :bot.

Entered through a storefront on the west side of Tenth Avenue between 26th and 27th streets, Glass inhabits a shaped cylinder that morphs all the way back to an open-air garden, via a glass gateway and accented with a stand of bamboo. Mildly referencing the 1960s, the main space feels like an extruded cyclorama, complete with a long banquette that drops down from the ceiling and egglike fiberglass chairs. In a departure from the hot pink, day-glo orange and chartreuse of :bot and Pod, the primary color scheme here is an urban camouflage of black, cool grey and white. Leeser's computer-aided formal concept is recreated in three-dimensional space with remarkable clarity and tactility. The mosaic of tiles prefacing the bathroom is rendered in a pattern mimetic of digital pixels, an illusion enhanced by curves in the plaster that erase the datum between floor, wall and ceiling.

As the type is all but dependent on the reproduction of effects, Glass' principal exterior conceit is a one-way mirror that allows people on the street to inspect club patrons as they preen in front of the bathroom sink. Drawing from an architectural trend in voyeuristic games most typified by the spectator-friendly changing areas at OMA's downtown Prada emporium (2001), and the bank of LCD screens that preview entering guests at Diller and Scofidio's midtown Brasserie (2000), Glass reverses the order of another unisex toilet—at Ogawa/Depardon's Bar 89 on Mercer Street (1995)—where the privacy of individuals using any one of the five clear-glass stalls is protected only by a sandwiched layer of liquid crystal that obscures the transparent enclosures on cue.

01. View of one-way mirror facing 10th Avenue.

02. Digital model of the shell housing the program.

03. View looking into the bar, from the outdoor
    garden in the back.

04. View towards the open-air garden along the
    axis of the banquette on the north wall.

Van Alen Institute

30 West 22nd Street
Lewis Tsurumaki Lewis
1998

06.

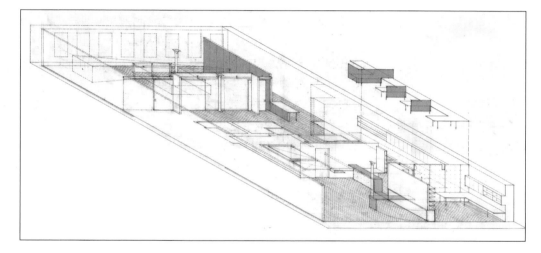

The renovation of the Van Alen Institute was designed to meet the diverse requirements of a think tank with a particular emphasis on civic architecture and urban design. With origins dating back to the late nineteenth century, the organization sponsors academic research and publications and annually hosts a number of exhibitions, lectures, and other public events within the space.

Lewis Tsurumaki Lewis' proposal was governed by two constraints: an existing loft space within a narrow, mid-block site, and a modest budget. The client mandated a design that would produce a coherent and legible organization of spaces, while allowing flexibility between the different programmatic components. Central to the project was a need to unify and demarcate the private office zone and the public gallery area.

The project was approached by strategically removing portions of the existing scheme. A single open gallery space was created by demolishing the walls, doors and ceilings that had previously divided the gallery into three compartmentalized areas. This allowed for the creation of a single uninterrupted display wall running the full depth of the building. Then a series of tactical elements were inserted into the modified context to maximize the possible functional configurations and operation of the space. These components were deployed to encourage multiple uses and readings of the space.

01. - 05. Views through the private office and public gallery. A sliding wall transforms the rear portion of the gallery into a space for lectures and symposia.

06. Axonometric diagram.

07.

08.

07. - 09. Operable Lumasite panels can be manipulated to produce changing degrees of closure for the director's office.

10. Detail of threshold. A steel ribbon mediates between public and private areas.

11. Part of the steel ribbon, the storage wall conceals a pivoting table for receptions.

12. Views of office.

09.

10.

11.

12.

Baruch College Vertical Campus

55 Lexington Avenue
Kohn Pedersen Fox
2001

02.

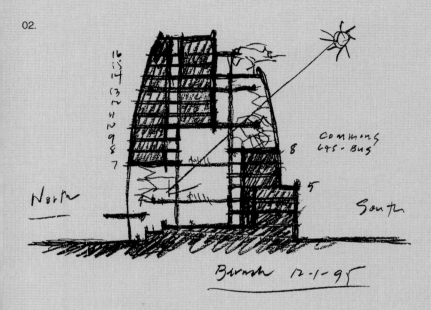

Occupying three-quarters of a city block, this building is designed as a vertical reinterpretation of a traditional college quadrangle. Located on Lexington Avenue and 25th Street and across the street from the recently completed Newman Library by Davis Brody Bond (1994), the "vertical campus" building doubles Baruch's existing classroom and administrative space while anchoring the college's urban campus.

At the heart of the building is a great central atrium that steps upward toward the sun, culminating in a giant square window on the south curtainwall that bathes the public spaces in natural light. This "quad" connects the three dominant building components: the liberal arts college, the business school, and the shared social amenities. The upper floors accommodate a variety of classrooms and offices that are linked by the atrium, which provides gathering places for students and faculty to interact. The lower and basement floors house large public assembly rooms and athletic facilities.

The massing and exterior wall systems address local zoning requirements and the scale of the surrounding neighborhood. Each elevation responds to the internal program and exterior context with a range of cladding materials and window sizes. The five-story brick and stone base relates directly to nearby buildings while the high-rise component is broken into parts—with varying layers of corrugated aluminum, ribbon windows and glass curtainwall defining each elevation.

Oversized windows frame the central atrium on the north facade and provide a visual connection to the Newman Library. Private offices on the perimeter have operable vents to regulate the flow of fresh air.

01. View to the east on 25th Street.

02. Sketch of section looking east.

03. Aerial view to the southeast, with Baruch in the center and the 25th Street Armory, foreground.

04. - 07. Entry sequence along 25th Street.

04.

05.

06.

07.

09.

08. View of the great
    room with the
    south-facing
    lounge on the
    eighth floor.

09. View looking up
    from the fifth floor.

10. Stairwell, sixth
    floor landing with
    custom lamps.

10.

Mosex

233 Fifth Avenue
Sharples Holden Pasquarelli
Design Completed 1999

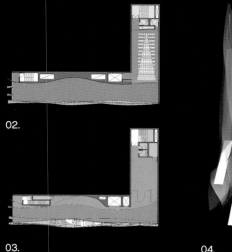

02.

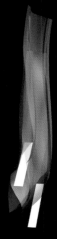

03.

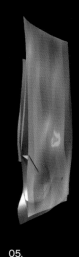

04.

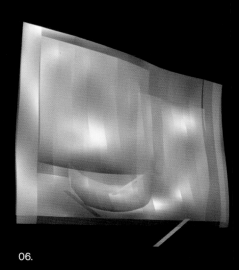

05.

06.

Currently housed in an interim exhibition space, the Museum of Sex is proposed for a narrow site on the northeast corner of Fifth Avenue and 27th Street. The stated mission of Mosex is to present a history of human sexuality and its generative role in culture and society. Accordingly, its directors selected a midtown address in recognition of New York City's inimitable role in shaping American attitudes about sex.

To shoehorn 40,000 square-feet of museum program into a tight footprint, the New York firm Sharples Holden Pasquarelli (ShoP) describes an efficient spatial logic, derived from "concepts of organic form, tactile expression, exposure and concealment," that ultimately supports an interpretation of the project as a kind of skin. In plan and section, this dermis is composed of layered strata that characterize the massing of the project

The materiality and arrangement of the wall systems address a brief for a light-filled museum program within a sculpted enclosure. The interior walls incorporate display volumes and mask essential infrastructure behind sweeping curves. An opalescent composition of glass and steel defines the facades, its layers compounded into a seamless expanse, or else split apart to permit light and vertical circulation. The levels of transparency on the curtainwall mimic a diaphanous dress, portrayed by its designers as a foil in a "flirtatious game" between the museum and the density of surrounding buildings. Clearly visible to passersby, the street level interior is a provocation: the museum visitor is seen as the final, participatory element in a formal exercise that is ultimately devoted to the gratification of desire.

01. Northeast corner, 27th and Fifth Avenue.

02. Roof plan.

03. Typical gallery plan.

04. - 06. Views along curtainwall "skin."

07. Aerial view, northeast corner.

07.

Scandinavia House

58 Park Avenue South
Polshek Partnership
2000

The American-Scandinavian Foundation has been promoting educational and cultural exchanges between the United States and the five Nordic countries—Denmark, Finland, Iceland, Norway, and Sweden—for nearly a century. In October 2000, the foundation moved to a new address on a mid-block site along Park Avenue, between 37th and 38th Streets.

Behind a facade of gray stone animated by horizontal openings and tapered wood shutters, Scandinavia House incorporates approximately 31,000 square-feet of cultural program in an eight-story townhouse. The center features a children's learning center, five exhibition galleries, an auditorium, a library, a meeting hall, conference and seminar rooms, a gift shop, and a café located to the left of main lobby with views of Park Avenue.

Designed by the Polshek Partnership, the center hosts an extensive calendar of events—encompassing everything from the visual and performing arts, to politics and business—and much of the program spaces are designed to showcase Scandinavian design and materials. This plays a major role in the experience of the center: Poulsen lamps, Jacobsen chairs and expanses of clear-finished birch wood are strategically used throughout the interior, most ubiquitously in the Victor Borge Hall, a 168-seat theater for performances and lectures, and the Halldór Laxness Library.

01. Interior view from the second floor landing of the narrow entrance atrium facing Park Avenue.

02. Facade on Park Avenue South.

03. Louis Poulsen's Artichoke lamps overlook the
atrium and the space for special events on
the second floor.

04. Scandinavia House's AQ Café is operated by
Restaurant Aquavit.

03.

04.

01. Model view of
    elevation facing
    avenue.

02. Perspective from
    the roofscape.

03. Model view of
    the roofscape
    along the street
    elevation.

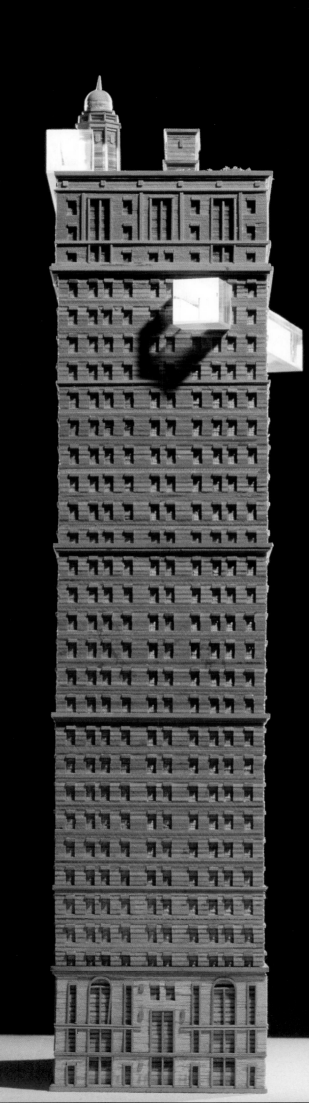

Manhattan Penthouse

Midtown
Tadao Ando
Design Completed 1997

This project by Osaka-based Tadao Ando called for the addition of a 7,600-square-foot penthouse and guesthouse to an existing midtown residential building from the 1920s. Ando apprehends the city as a unified whole despite its many architecturally distinct parts and accordingly put forth a singular residential concept that "captured the city as it is, but without yielding to the city's heterogeneous energies."

The intervention consists of a steel-and-concrete frame enveloped by a skin of glass, precariously set along the north axis of the building roof. This metaphysical feat—a mass appearing to float in the air—is repeated some five floors down by another construct

of similar form and materiality. Only this time, the glass box is not so much inserted, but jammed aslant into the brick and terracotta hide of the older building.

The scheme also includes a theatrical landscape in the form of a rooftop aerie complete with plantings and a watercourse, a platform from which the residents of the penthouse can view the skyline of the city. By contrasting an early Manhattan skyscraper with a contemporary architectural idiom of steel, aggregate and glass, Ando hoped to create a city in miniature, one that constantly "draws inspiration from the mixture of the new and the old."

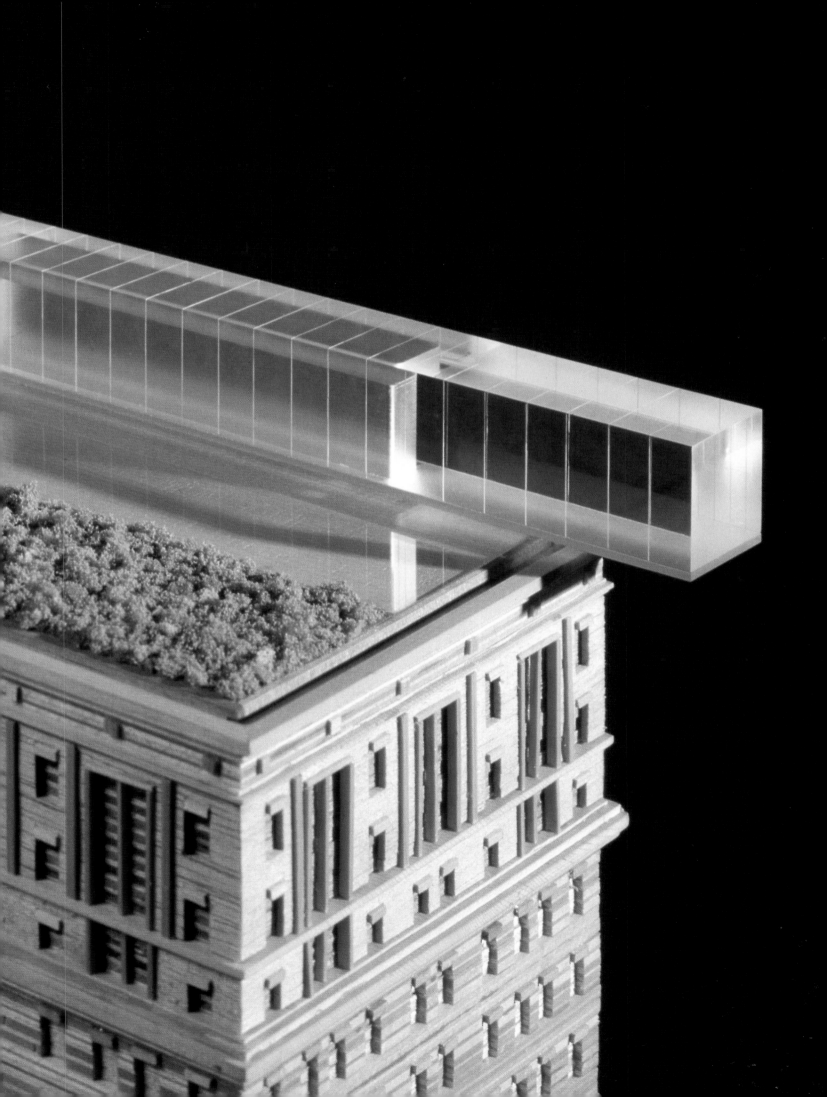

425 Fifth Avenue

425 Fifth Avenue
Michael Graves Architect
2003

Located on the northeast corner of Fifth Avenue and 38th Street in midtown, this mixed-use 300,000-square-foot tower houses fifty-six floors, ascending to a height of over six hundred feet. The building's massing reconciles New York City zoning regulations with the unusually small footprint of its site.

Set on a narrow 150-by-77-foot lot, the building's six-story commercial plinth contains two floors of retail and four floors of offices. The scale and detailing of the limestone and glass base respond to historically significant low-rise buildings in the immediate neighborhood along Fifth Avenue.

Referencing its iconic neighbors, the slender tower sets back three times as it rises, beginning on the seventh floor, which houses residential amenities and a public terrace that wraps around the building. The eighth floor contains an extensive business center as well as a lounge for the Envoy Club, an extended-stay residence that rises through the twenty-sixth floor. Higher floors contain a variety of luxury condominium apartments, with floor plates ranging from 5,900 square-feet on the lower residential floors to 3,100 square-feet on the upper levels.

Using a bright palette of materials, the contemporary facade accentuates the building's height with alternating vertical bands of tan and white brick. Blue louvers and window mullions separate tall casement windows that rise to a height just below the ceiling level of each floor.

01. View along Fifth Avenue.

01.

02.

New York Public Library
Science, Industry & Business Library

188 Madison Avenue
Gwathmey Siegel Architects
1996

Occupying five levels of the landmark B. Altman building on 34th Street between Fifth and Madison avenues, the 250,000-square-foot Science, Industry and Business Library (SIBL) was the New York Public Library's largest construction project in the 1990s. Emphasizing accessibility and flexibility to accommodate new technology, the design transforms the former department store into the NYPL system's most advanced multimedia resource.

Large street-level windows on Madison Avenue invite pedestrians into a two-story atrium, created by removing a portion of the existing first floor. The atrium converts the basement level into a bright 44,000-square-foot space for reading and exhibitions.

One hundred computer workstations provide free access to the Internet and other electronic research tools, while five hundred more workstations use adjustable perforated dividers to create flexible personal space for laptop use. Stone and wood join stainless steel and terrazzo throughout the facility to convey the institution's tradition and its demonstrated ability to adapt to change.

SIBL houses an open-shelf reference collection, periodical and microfilm shelving, catalog areas, reading areas, an electronic information center, a training center, assembly spaces, and 50,000 square-feet of administrative offices. 60,000 square-feet of remote storage stacks hold 1.5 million volumes, and a full-service circulation library contains 60,000 volumes

Unobstructed sight lines allow the library to be supervised by a small security staff, freeing librarians to focus on research and consulting with patrons. SIBL staff areas surround the stacks on the second through fourth floors, while the three uppermost levels are used for general New York Public Library administration.

Other tenants in the renovated building include the CUNY Graduate Center (also by Gwathmey Siegel) and the New York offices of Oxford University Press.

01. Interior view, street level.

02. Interior view, lower level.

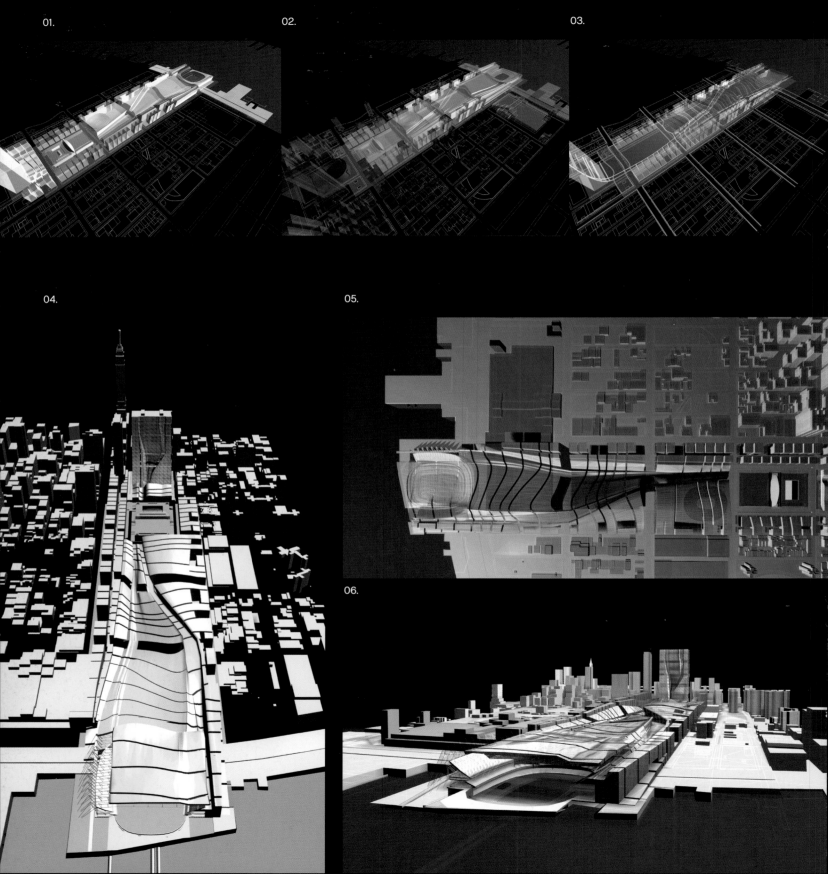

01.

02.

03.

04.

05.

06.

IFCCA Prize Competition for the Design of Cities

West Side
Eisenman Architects
Design Completed 1999

Sponsored by the International Foundation for the Canadian Center for Architecture (IFCCA), this is the first of a series of international competitions to be held every three years in cities around the world. Offering a prize of $100,000, the IFCCA selected as its first site an isolated 3.5 million square-foot area bounded by Eighth Avenue, 30th Street, 34th Street and the Hudson River on the West Side of Manhattan. Juried by a panel of six architects, the official participation of the chairpersons of both the City Planning Commission and the New York State Development Corporation suggests that at least some of the ideas generated by the contest will make it into the final master plan.

Peter Eisenman's first=prize entry proposes the development of a high-density horizontal intervention fostering low-rise commercial and residential development while introducing public open space laterally into the city rather than just along the river's edge. Through landscaping and programming, it integrates the river with the city's interior while offering regional and local transit systems new access to the far West Side.

Weaving large-scale public attractions into the urban fabric, the design presents a series of public amenities, including parkland, shopping, schools and hotels, as an integrated whole. The project's programmed spaces—such as stadium and convention center—form a continuous fabric of public urban and park space. By expanding the Jacob K. Javits Convention Center, extending subsurface transportation connections, and adding hotels, shopping and media centers, the design establishes the West Side as a magnet for tourists as well as the commercial and residential tenants who will invigorate the neighborhood.

The design plays on the traditional view of buildings as figural objects on neutral ground, positing instead a figure/figure relationship. Through interplay of gridded urban space and a new smooth space, the concept blurs the figure/ground distinction between building and context. The ground—formerly a flat datum—is warped to make it figural. Sectional space between building objects meets the new ground, and the intersection of these two figures creates an activated interstitial space. On the southern edge, cuts in the warped figural surface of the ground form subtractive voids, allowing the gridded space to reveal the presence of a formerly hidden smooth space, and the smooth space, when cut away, to reveal a gridded space.

01. - 03. Diagram sequence illustrating major programmatic elements and circulation plan. Views from Seventh Avenue to Hudson River.

04. View to east.

05. Aerial view of 24-block site.

06. View looking into waterfront stadium.

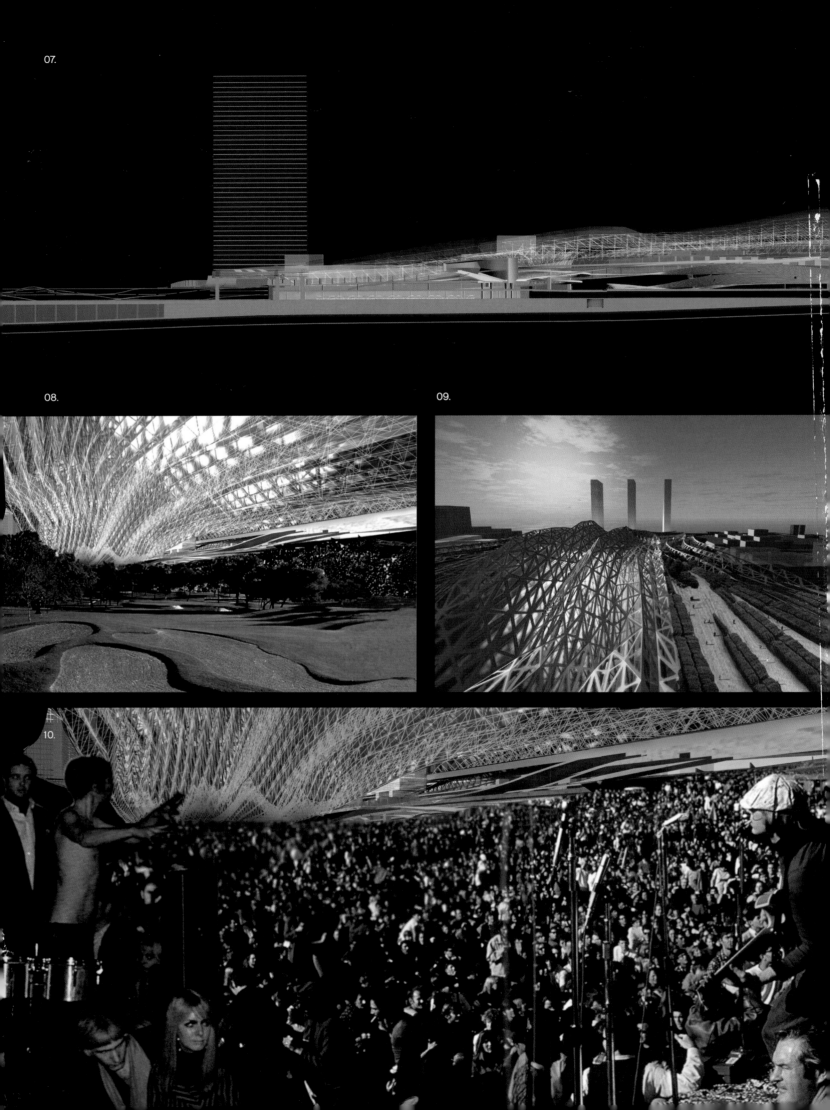

07.

08.

09.

10.

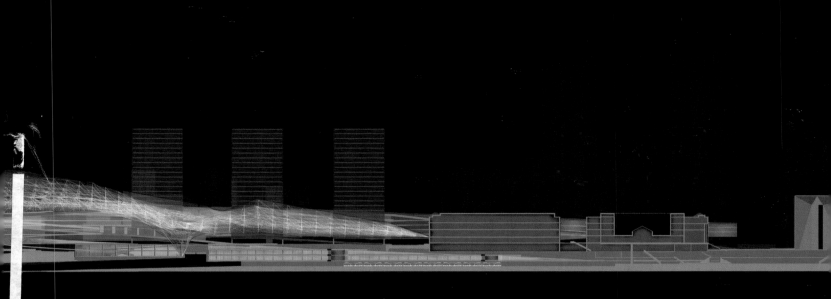

West Side
Reiser + Umemoto RUR Architecture
Design Completed 1999

Along with winning entrant Eisenman Architects, Reiser + Umemoto RUR Architecture was the other Manhattan-based firm that made it to the final round of the IFCCA's inaugural Prize Competition for the Design of Cities. Principals Jesse Reiser and Nanako Umemoto reinvent the site by bridging the gap separating the diverse programmatic components of a large urban master plan. Immersed within a large park space, this assemblage blends elements that would traditionally remain distinct and isolated to produce a zone of constant activity. Not only does the design contain multiple uses, it also creates flows that mix and unite them.

The proposal provides for a needed extension of the Jacob K. Javits Convention Center, while connecting and relating its functions to the neighborhood and facilities around it, including a new museum, concert hall, a performance hall and an Imax theater. The design includes several civic, cultural and leisure amenities, all within close proximity and sharing a common mezzanine.

Varied park and landscape settings, with vast yet articulated surfaces, are woven throughout the site for recreation, sport and leisure use. Located above a rail yard and beneath a continuous but differentiated glass-and-steel canopy, this event space seems at once inside and outside. Sports can be played as in an outdoor park while large concerts requiring protection from the elements are possible year-round. The green space also serves residents of adjacent neighborhoods and connects those neighborhoods to the Hudson River.

The numerous retail components make the site a prominent shopping destination and help maintain pedestrian traffic on weekends. The retail elements continue east into Penn Station, where stores placed along commuter corridors provoke more complex use of public space. The design includes elevated parking for drivers, while ferry terminals at Pier 79 provide access to New Jersey and other points in Manhattan.

07. Site section from west to east.

08. View of covered greenspace.

09. View looking west.

10. The great roof as a venue for performances.

Daniel Patrick Moynihan Station

Eighth Avenue, 31st-33rd Street
Skidmore, Owings & Merrill
Design Completed 1998

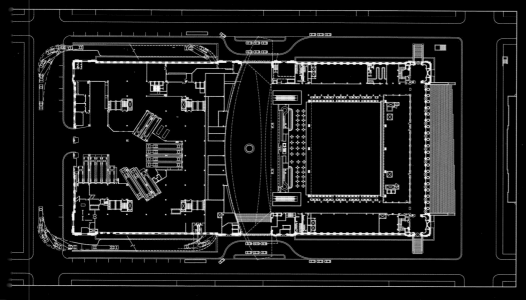

02.

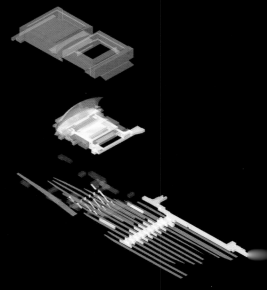

03.

"In the old time, you arrived at Pennsylvania Station at the train platform, you went up the stairs to heaven. Make that Manhattan. And we shall have it again. Praise all."

Senator Daniel Patrick Moynihan, October 2002

The planned $500-million conversion of the James A. Farley Post Office Building into a modern transportation center will stand as a tribute to a highly personal crusade led by the late U.S. Senator from New York, Daniel Patrick Moynihan, to atone for what he called "the great act of vandalism in the history of the city." Completed in 1914, the Farley Building stood across from the original Pennsylvania Station—then the grandest rail terminal in all of North America—until it was demolished in 1963 to make way for the fourth (and certainly the most reviled) incarnation of Madison Square Garden.

This current project—orchestrated through the agency of the Empire State Development Corporation and its subsidiary, the Pennsylvania Station Redevelopment Corporation—will start construction with the purchase of the existing structure from the United States Postal Service, and is expected to open in 2008.

Skidmore, Owings & Merrill's (SOM) scheme for the 1.4 million-square-foot facility preserves much of the civic character of the McKim, Mead and White design, as it carves out a twenty-first-century terminal for high-speed train links within the building's enormous shell. The landmarked postal hall facing Eighth Avenue, as well as essential postal operations along Ninth Avenue, are retained.

To mark the transition between the new station and the still-extensive post office functions,

01. 33rd Street entrance, looking south.

02. Ground floor plan.

03. Exploded axonometric: Post office functions (top); station and retail (middle); mechanical and circulation (bottom).

04. View looking west.

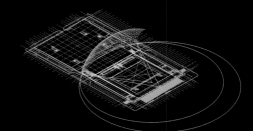

on the western half of the complex, SOM devised a mid-block ticketing hall, tented by a 150-foot high spherical section truss. A delicate, light-filled counterpoint to the symmetrical mass of the Farley Building, this glass-and-steel enclosure will open at both ends to support the station's new entrances on 31st and 33rd Streets. A new train concourse—evocative of the great room of the martyred station—will be created within the Farley Building's existing courtyard. The hall's restored skylights will allow light down from and views up to the city from the train platforms, referencing another one of old Penn Station's defining experiences.

The new entry sequence will lend the Moynihan Station a monumentality appropriate for what is hoped will again become the busiest transport hub on the eastern seaboard, conveying travelers on a new generation of intercity rail lines. There are plans to connect the "air-trains" servicing Newark, LaGuardia and JFK airports through Moynihan Station, and the more optimistic proposals even suggest airline ticketing and flight-information services inside the concourse, an amenity common to a growing list of cities outside the United States. A tall order, certainly, but new Penn Station (and it will remain Penn Station to a great many) at least promises that alighting passengers won't ever have to scuttle into the city like rats.

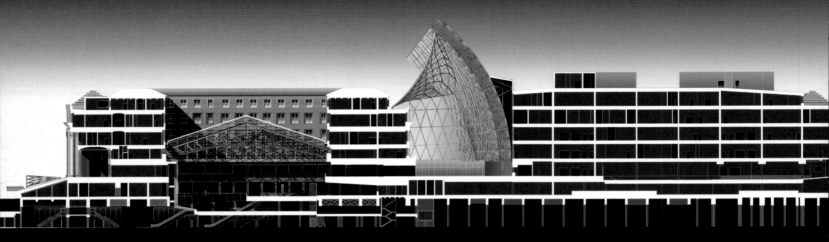

09. Section looking south.

10. Platform for high-speed trains. View to west.

Miller / Jones Studio

Garment District
Lot/ek
1996

Breathing new life to discarded industrial objects and household appliances, the hunter-scavenger pair of Giuseppe Lignano and Ada Tolla—who together make up the architecture firm Lot/ek—engaged in a number of residential explorations in New York City during the mid-to-late 1990s. Arguably the most successful of these was their first mature work: a commission to design an appropriately dramatic space for a scenographer and a fashion photographer to live and work in. This involved the rapid conversion of a commercial loft on the 14th floor of a building in west midtown, with high ceilings, southern exposure and a thrity-foot window that offers panoramic views of the city.

For their principal actor, Lot/ek salvaged the side of a 40-foot aluminum shipping container from the junkyard, tore it off its trailer bed,

spiffed it up a bit (they left most of its stenciled freight markings and enameled decals in place), and set it along the diagonal axis of the former warehouse. In utilizing the lightweight metal shell, the architects effectively divided the loft into zones for living and working. The surface of the wall is cut out to support separate functions within the container itself, and a system of operable panels is fashioned out of the aluminum skin. When these revolving doors are swung open, the contents of the truck—bedroom, bathroom and kitchen—are united with the more public workspaces. Four old refrigerators are laid on their sides, bolted together and mounted on casters to form a movable workstation. The doors open to reveal necessary technologies (scanner, computer and printer), and wood tops pull out to create tables.

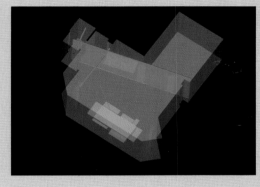

03.

04.

05.

01.

02.

42nd Street Now!

Times Square
Robert A. M. Stern Architects
M&Co.
1993

The ongoing redevelopment of Times Square had an uneasy and protracted genesis. The hive of construction and activity that has characterized the neighborhood since the mid 1990s is essentially a reaction to a particularly controversial plan by Philip Johnson and John Burgee in 1984 to replace the warren of adult movie theaters and peepshow parlors on 42nd Street and Seventh Avenue with four bleak office towers. Exceedingly unpopular, the scheme was abandoned in the early 1990s.

In its wake, a more dynamic (but no less contentious) vision for 42nd Street quietly took shape. Conceived, funded and managed through the agency of the state, the city and other invited private actors, the new plan was the most ambitious building program ever proposed for the area. Its authors were not interested in merely papering over forty years of squalor or adding several million square-feet of Class-A office space. To lure back tourists, a key objective of the project was nothing less than a restoration—or at least an approximation—of the vibrant street life that had been associated with the area since the nineteenth century. To this end, two consummate showmen—the architect, historian and educator Robert A. M. Stern and the late Tibor Kalman of the influential graphic design firm M&Co.—were brought in by the New York State Urban Development

Corporation (UDC) and the New York City Economic Development Corporation to produce an interim plan and signage guidelines. The 42nd Street Development Corporation—the UDC proxy running the Times Square project—in consultation with the board of the recently established Times Square Business Improvement District (BID), unveiled "42nd Street Now!" in 1993.

Limited to key sites within a thirteen-acre tract between Seventh and Eighth avenues nicknamed "the deuce," the interim scheme was devised to bring flash—and generate the conditions for a very big bang. It called for the rapid construction of provisional structures and event-generators to dress up existing lots while tenants for more permanent edifices were lined up. With complementary businesses at their base, the first of these temporary sites was set up in 1995, many complete with illuminated displays several stories high. The signage guidelines that dictated the scale and placement of supergraphics for this test phase, and for all future development, were crucial. The instant cut-out city that the new standards mandated into existence effectively broadcast the potential of the newly empowered BID. In three years, practically all of these placeholders had served their purpose; with the lots parceled out all

were ultimately destined for the skyscrapers that now occupy them.

From this perspective, the interim plan fared better than some of its critics anticipated. In an unprecedented experiment in globalization, some of the old gray men of Wall Street have even vacated their downtown premises to join the U.S. Armed Forces, the Disney Vacation Club, E-Walk, the New Amsterdam Theater, MTV, Suntory Whiskey, the Virgin Megastore, Ruby Foos, the Royalton, the Paramount, Hello Kitty, the NBC Jumbotron, and Madame Tussaud's to create a mixed-use mélange second to none on the planet. Moving into new, gleaming skyscrapers, the occupants of these august financial services giants may yet draw some of that old-time seaminess back to 42nd Street—inadvertently, of course—and finally deliver something for everybody.

Incidentally, the quartet of towers that now occupy key sites inside the lower bowtie of Times Square—two by Fox and Fowle, one each by KPF and SOM—all exceed the Johnson-Burgee proposals in height and floor-to-area ratio (FAR) largely because they are state-regulated projects and are therefore excluded from the maximum FAR allotted by the City Planning Commission.

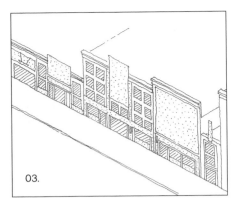

03.

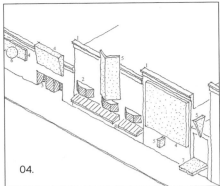

04.

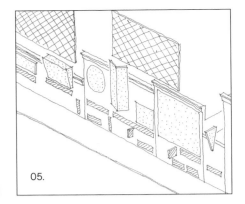

05.

06.

Preceding pages:

01. Suggested build-out: south side of 42nd Street,
near Seventh Avenue, looking east.

02. Interim structures: 42nd Street, looking east,
late 1996.

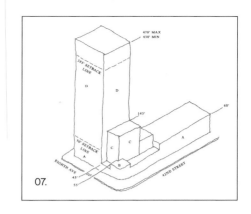

07.

03. Suggested window and signage treatment.

04. Suggested three-dimensional elements.

05. Illustrative signage categories.

06. Northwest corner, 42nd Street and Seventh Avenue, interim scheme.

07. Building height and setback criteria.

08. Suggested build-out: northeast 42nd Street and Eighth Avenue.

Four Times Square

Four Times Square
Fox and Fowle
1999

Fully occupying the northeast corner of 42nd Street and Broadway, Four Times Square is the first office tower to be built under the agency of the 42nd Street Development Corporation established by the New York State Urban Development Corporation. The construction of the 48-story building marked a turning point in the mission of the Times Square BID, accelerating the tempo of massive development within the "bowtie" formed by the intersection of Broadway and Seventh Avenue. Commissioned by the Durst Organization, most of its 1.6 million square-feet was eventually let to the Condé Nast publishing empire, which had managed to make the most out of a climate of intense media consolidation in the mid-to-late 1990s.

Fox and Fowle envisaged a tower with two distinct facades, each intended as contextual responses to two primary conditions. The west and north elevations appropriate the mixed-use character of New Times Square and are clad primarily in metal and glass; the masonry walls on the east facade and the southern 42nd Street exposure were devised for the more corporate environment east of Sixth Avenue and Bryant Park. The result is a sequence of interlocking setbacks and facade treatments that address the diverse scale and character of the neighboring buildings. As the tower rises, the collage of volumes briefly evolves into an integrated composition of reflective glass some 35 stories above ground before terminating into a mannered tangle of steel rigging. This articulated top supports a communications tower and was originally intended to frame sixty-foot signs.

The project is also seen as a nascent expression of environmental responsibility. It is the first project of its size to set new standards for energy conservation, indoor air quality and the use of sustainable materials. Four Times Square's nonrenewable energy consumption is a thirty to forty percent less than that of a conventional building built in the 1980s. Efficient building services recirculate fresh air into the building at five times the New York State energy code minimum, and procedures were established for maintaining the building systems at optimal levels. The building also generates five percent of its own electricity. Photovoltaic panels have been substituted for the typical spandrel panels on the upper floors of the east and south facades, and the fuel cells generate additional electricity for the building.

01. View looking south.

02.

03.

02. View of the
southwest corner,
looking up from
42nd Street.

03. Building entry on
the northeast
corner of 42nd
Street and
Broadway.

04. View from Fifth
Avenue, with Bryant
Park to the left, and
to the right, the
upward sweep of
Gordon Bunshaft's
Grace Building
(1974).

08.

Locator map on page 182.

This sequence includes four of the towers built on or proposed for key sites along 42nd Street between Seventh and Eighth avenues. Four Times Square was the first building of this group to be completed.

05. Reuters Building
Three Times Square
Fox and Fowle
2003

06. Ernst and Young
Five Times Square
Kohn Pedersen Fox
2002

07. The Westin New York
42nd Street and
Eighth Avenue
Arquitectonica
2004 Completion

08 Port Authority Tower
41st - 42nd streets
and Eighth Avenue
Skidmore, Owings
& Merrill (SOM)
Design completed 1999

The New Victory Theater

209 West 42nd Street
Hardy Holzman Pfeiffer Associates
1995

02.

Opened in December 1995, the renovated New Victory Theater represents the first permanent construction within the stretch of 42nd Street between Seventh and Eighth avenues, the core of the redevelopment project managed by the New York State Urban Development Corporation. Built as the Republic Theater by Oscar Hammerstein in 1900, it is one of the city's oldest performance spaces, and after spending most of the last three decades in an x-rated limbo, the New 42nd Street Inc. earmarked it as the pilot project for an aggressive campaign to rehabilitate seven of the neighborhood's fabled playhouses.

The theater's most recent incarnation offers one of the more interesting year-round programs of any theater in the city, mixing innovative, youth-oriented fare with short-run engagements by traveling repertories such as the Shakespeare's New Globe Theater. To restore the Victory, Hardy Holzman Pfeiffer

Associates had to tear out nearly a century of provisional architectural modifications. The updated program consists of an expanded lobby and basement, and the addition of an upper lobby. The original brownstone stoop is recreated with a grand double stair and ornate lampposts, and parts of the exterior brickwork refaced. In the interior, the intricate plaster moldings and woodwork were brought back, along with the faux drapery, a host of putti and elaborate theater boxes on either side of the stage. The bumblebee, laurel leaf and fleur-de-lis motifs, evidenced by historical photographs, reappear variously as patterns on walls, wrought-iron stanchions and upholstery.

With vastly improved lighting and acoustics, the theater now incorporates all the necessary technologies of a modern theater. The scheme also inserts an elevator, upgrades the stage-fly, and renovates an existing infill structure to accommodate support functions.

01. Interior view.
The elaborate theater boxes were restored.

02. View along 42nd Street, 1995.

New 42nd Street Studios

225-229 West 42nd Street
Platt Byard Dovell White
1999

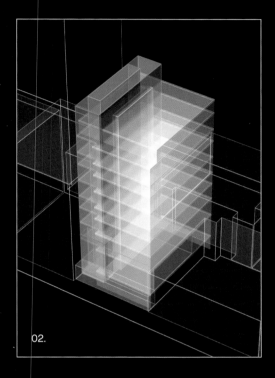

02.

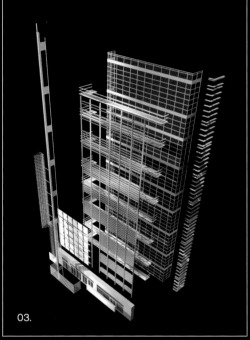

03.

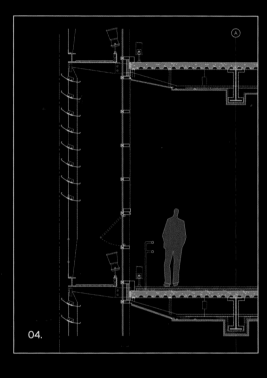

04.

Designed by the Manhattan firm of Platt Byard Dovell White in 1997 (then just Platt Byard Dovell), the New 42nd Street Studios was commissioned by The New 42nd Inc., the nonprofit trust in charge of resurrecting six of the historic theaters within the Times Square redevelopment project. Inserted mid-block on the north side of 42nd Street between Seventh and Eighth avenues, the building serves as a "creative factory" for the performing arts, with 84,000 square-feet of program distributed to a dozen rehearsal rooms, two hybrid studio and reception areas, a 199-seat "black box" experimental theater—The Duke on 42nd Street—and dressing rooms and other support functions for the dance companies and acting ensembles that utilize it. The modern facility hosts a retail base on 42nd Street, and a through-block connection to the Selwyn on 43rd Street rechristened the American Airlines Theater in 1999.

The lighting strategy employed on the building exterior reinterprets the rigorous standards set up by the 42nd Street Corporation for external signage and provides a solution consistent to the letter and spirit of the mandated guidelines. In place of conventional neon-illuminated billboards, the building's facade is a collage of metal and glass, with reflective dichroic glass at the base, a 175-foot-high "Light Pipe," and an array of perforated metal blades that refract an infinitely variable display of colored lights projected from rows of programmable theatrical lamps. Behind the steel screen, the transparent glass curtain-wall further animates the exterior, filtering out light from within the rehearsal rooms and the movement of the dancers themselves.

01. View from west.

02. Stacking diagram.

03. Exploded view. Curtainwall components.

04. Detail view of wall section.

05. Detail of curtainwall,
with perforated
steel screens.

06. Interior of studio,
looking out to
42nd Street.

07. Detail: dichroic
glass panels.

08. View of 199-seat
"black box" theater.

08.

01.

NISSIN FOODS

Budweiser

New York Time

17 : 03 : 22

Budweiser

Panasonic

TDK

AUDIO AND VIDEO CASSETTES

AS
SERIOUS
AS
YOU
CAN
GET

JOE BOXER

Cab a ni

100% of the fares from the
Chevy Venture – JOE BOXER
cab goes to ConceptCure
for breast cancer research.
Want to help?
Hail it today or call:
1-888-GM-CCURE

Chevy Venture

Help
stamp
our
breast
cancer!

THE
GREEN MILE

POKÉMON
The Movie

NOVEMBER 12

New York Police Dept

FedEx
Federal

BEAUTY of the BEAST

U.S. Armed Forces Recruiting Station

West 43rd Street
Architectural Research Office
1999

Harnessing the iconic power of Times Square, the US Armed Forces first set up a temporary conscription and recruitment facility on 43rd Street during World War II. This new 520-square-foot station—designed by Stephen Cassell and Adam Yarinsky of ARO—replaces the first permanent structure built on the site in 1946 and shares similar footprint and height requirements. It sits atop an existing subway ventilation grille on a narrow traffic median inside the lower "bowtie" created by Seventh Avenue and Broadway. The building houses a modest program of four desks, one for each of the four armed services—Army, Navy, Air Force, Marines, and a bathroom.

Dwarfed by its soaring neighbors, the east and west facades of the diminutive structure display two large illuminated American flags. The motif of a flag, its unmistakable symbolic properties maximized to breeze through a complicated approval process, achieves a more elaborate meaning in the context of its site. Reflecting the surrounding signage, the flags are fully integrated into Times Square, at once a direct appeal to patriotic duty and a commercial advertisement for a military now wholly dependent on volunteers. This nuanced interpretation of the project, owing chiefly to its extraordinary location, is unusual for governmental buildings. Every aspect of the design emphasizes the flags which are made of fluorescent lamps sandwiched between the building's steel frame and glazed exterior. The individual light fixtures are sheathed within a translucent membrane, through which the red, white, and blue are visible throughout the day, and protected from the elements by large panes of glass.

The south elevation serves as a brassard for four ornate service emblems, set against a twenty-foot-high backdrop of aluminum grates. Hidden behind this porous metal skin are conduits for water and electricity, steps leading to the roof, and a door to the controls of the Baccarat crystal ball that heralds New Year's Eve in Times Square. The window mullions are fashioned out of stainless steel, dulled to a soft sheen. The cross-section of the structure permits roof access and eliminates the need for a handrail. Internally, this profile is expressed through a dropped ceiling, creating a reflective white surface that enhances the reading of the flag from the street.

01. View looking south. The recruitment center stands in front of the sign-encrusted shell of One Times Square. Visible from the surrounding skyscrapers, the roof is painted an urban camouflage pattern of gray, black, and white.

177

02.

03.

02. View of entry on the north-facing elevation.

03. The interior features four desks for each of the armed services.

04. View looking north to the "bowtie" formed by Broadway and Seventh Avenue.

01.

02.

03.

745 Seventh Avenue

745 Seventh Avenue
Kohn Pedersen Fox
2001

This build-to-suit office tower, originally designed for Morgan Stanley Dean Witter and later sold to Lehman Brothers, is located between 49th and 50th Streets, on the western edge of Rockefeller Center and at the northern perimeter of Times Square. The last parcel of Rockefeller properties to be developed, the building uses a variety of curtainwall elements to mediate between the adjacent neighbor-hoods and create a vibrant streetscape.

The building is at the upper extremity of the Midtown Theater Subdistrict, which extends south to 40th Street and east to Sixth Avenue, and the signage guidlines amended by the City Planning Commission in 1987 suggest a signage program in keeping with the character of the neighborhood.

The tower rises through a series of setbacks that maximize floor area while complying with stringent New York City sky exposure require-ments. Windows alternate on the facade with continuous granite mullions in a vertical gesture drawn from Wallace K. Harrison's XYZ towers of Sixth Avenue and the core buildings of Rockefeller Center just beyond. This pattern

is broken at the southwest corner, where the glass and metal cladding transmits the building's internal lighting, contributing to the Times Square light show.

The building's podium incorporates a block-long illuminated display within the curtainwall. Three horizontal LED bands alternate with two floors of office windows and are joined above the building's entrance by an integrated forty-foot-tall LED billboard. In addition, the original proposal envisaged a map of the world rising another eighty feet. This changing and dynamic display, with a size unprecedented for its type makes an unequivocal connection with the building along the "bowtie" intersections created by Seventh Avenue and Broadway to the heart of Times Square.

The ground floor contains separate entrances on Seventh Avenue and on 49th and 50th Streets. It houses retail space, two generous lobbies, a porte-cochere, a garden plaza, a subway entrance, and a subsurface pedestrian connection from the 49th Street subway station to Rockefeller Plaza.

01. View looking east to Rockefeller Center.

02. Northeast corner, of 49th Street and Seventh Avenue.

03. The block-long, three-story LED display along Seventh Avenue.

04.

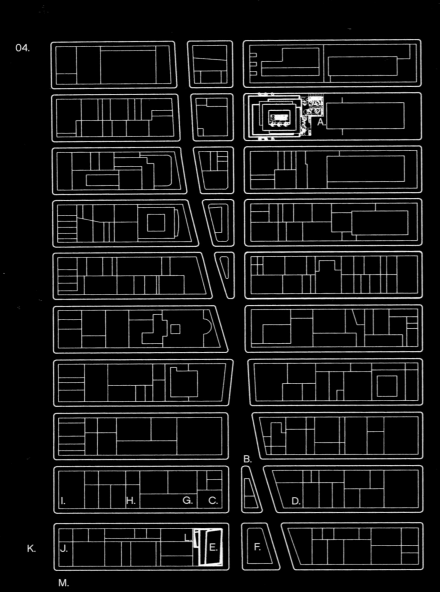

04. Locator map of Times Square

A. 745 Seventh Avenue (Kohn Pedersen Fox).

B. US Armed Forces Recruitment Center.
(Architectural Research Office).

C. Three Times Square (Fox and Fowle).

D. Four Times Square (Fox and Fowle).

E. Five Times Square (Kohn Pedersen Fox).

F. Ten Times Square ((Skidmore, Owings & Merrill).

G. New Victory Theater (Hardy Holzman Pfeiffer).

H. 42nd Street Studios (Platt Byard Dovell White).

I. The Westin New York on 42nd Street
(Arquitectonica).

J. Eleven Times Square (Fox and Fowle).

K. Port Authority Tower (Skidmore, Owings & Merrill).

L. New York Times Tower (Renzo Piano).

M. New Amsterdam Theater
(Hardy Holzman Pfeiffer).

05. 745 Seventh Avenue. View of lantern with
Wallace K. Harrison's XYZ buildings (1971-73)
in the background.

New York Times

40-41st Streets and Eighth Avenue
Renzo Piano Building Workshop
Fox and Fowle
Design Completed 2000

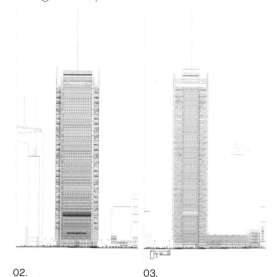

02.   03.

This design, by the Genoa and Paris-based Renzo Piano, was the winner of a much-publicized competition held by the 153-year-old newspaper for a new midtown headquarters. The planned 1.5 million-square-foot tower—on 40th and 41st Streets and Eighth Avenue—will stand on the southwestern flank of the Times Square BID, across from the Port Authority Bus Terminal and two blocks south of the Westin Hotel on 42nd Street. Upon completion, the New York Times will vacate its current, low-rise location off 7th Avenue and 43rd Street.

The architect proposed a narrative for the 52-story building different from that of its neighbors. Unlike the proposed tower planned to surmount the Port Authority Tower or the built forest of skyscrapers (3, 4, 5 and 10 Times Square) to the east, the Times Tower will not utilize reflective or tinted glass. Themes of transparency and lightness are central to the concept, and vast expanses of clear glass combined with a scrim of thin ceramic cylinders arranged in front of the

panes dominate the entire length of the curtainwall. In addition to twenty-eight elevators, its occupants can use stairs located along the facades, their movements visible to the street.

The metaphor of transparency is particularly valuable to a broadsheet widely touted as the country's newspaper of record. An open lobby carries the idea of clear expression further; with the principal building entry on busy Eighth Avenue, the lobby activates the street with the inclusion of shops, restaurant and a semipublic auditorium.

The crucial functions of the newspaper, namely its newsroom and its various editorial departments, are actually located on the upper stories of a low podium that extends from the slab of the tower east to the middle of the block. Overlooking the street, the office volumes along the perimeter of this extension embrace an interior garden accessible to the public.

01. Wast elevation, detail.

02. West elevation, along Eighth Avenue.

03. South elevation, along 40th Street.

04.

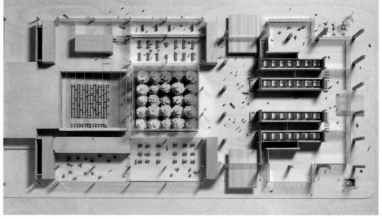

05.

04. Model view of 41st Street facade.

05. Model of the ground floor. The main entry on Eighth Avenue faces west, and the auditorium and public garden are oriented to the east.

06. The top of the tower with the proposed roof garden.

06.

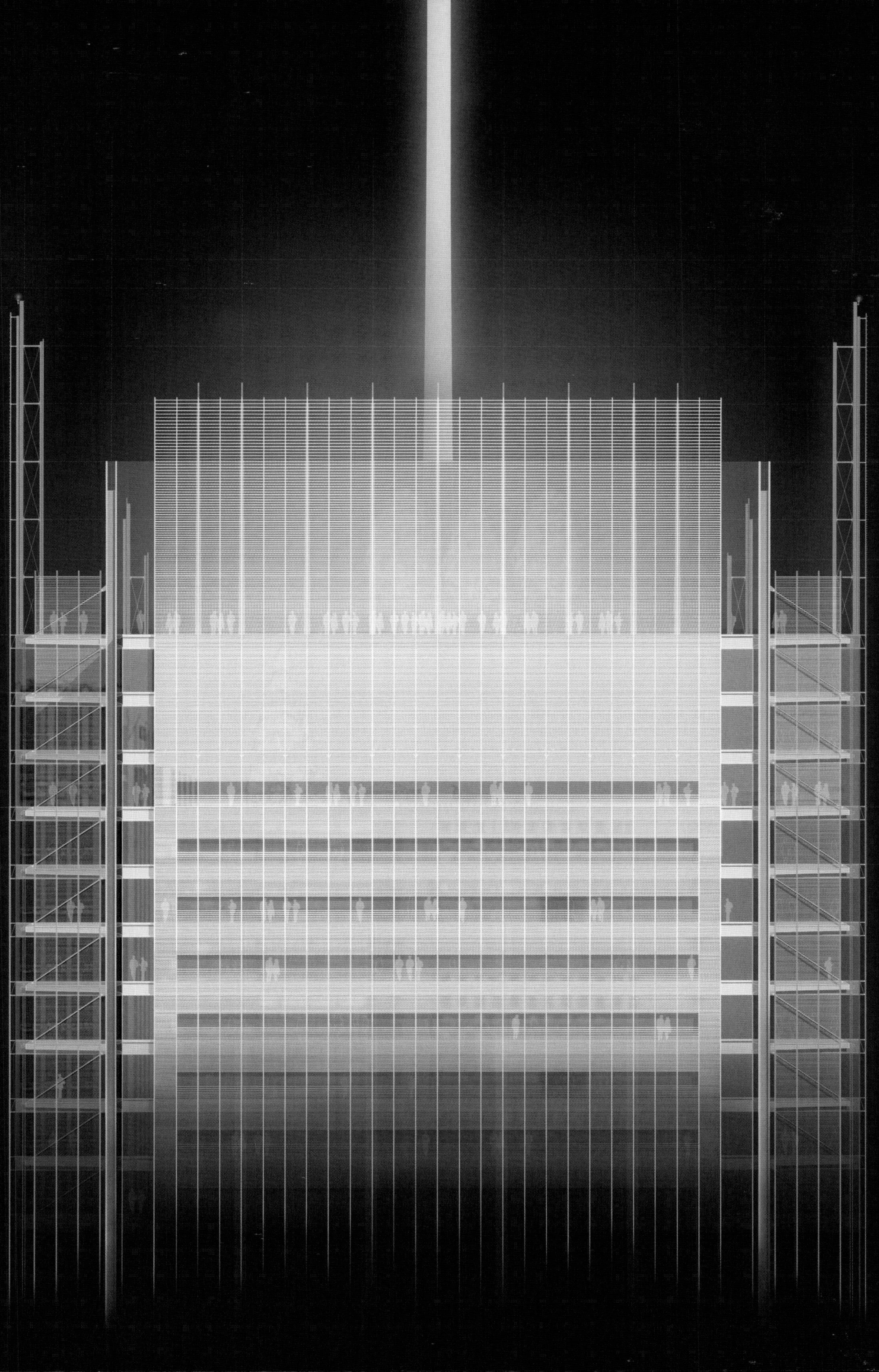

01.

02.

03.

04.

THAT
CHAMPIONSHIP
SEASON

05.

2econd
Stage
Theatre

2econd Stage Theater

307 West 43rd Street
Office for Metropolitan Architecture
Gluckman Mayner Architects
1999

06.

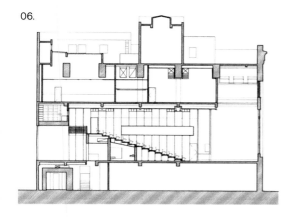

The brief for this project, a collaborative effort between the Office for Metropolitan Architecture and Gluckman Mayner Architects, required the conversion—on a comparatively tight budget—of an existing bank building into a new theater. Located on the western edge of Times Square, the new performing arts theater comprises 17,000 square-feet of program, supporting a 297-seat gallery, rehearsal space, dressing rooms and offices.

Access to the theater is through a first floor lobby along 43rd Street, where the theater's box office occupies the existing bank vault. The design preserves the spatial character of the existing building, achieving its transition to a playhouse through a number of key interventions. The second floor orchestra, a 6,000-square-foot space with 24-foot-high ceilings, remains untouched save for the insertion of a single wedge. It accommodates the seating, defines the lobby and stage, and contains the lavatories. Along the balcony, a translucent plastic wall permits the passage of actors and disguises mechanical functions without dividing the space. A removed section of the third floor allows for a fly loft—a high working platform to which scenery and lanterns are attached above the stage, maximizing operational flexibility and increasing the available height of the stage to 43 feet.

The third floor incorporates dressing rooms, wardrobe, green room and a column-free rehearsal area. The design introduces new materials into the interior. The seating wedge finish is sheathed in a textured epoxy resin: the exterior of the wedge painted blue-green, and underneath a bright orange. The theater seating combines wood chairs fitted with ergonomic gel cushions. A silver quilted acoustic blanket wraps the control booth and folds onto the ceiling of the theater, providing sound absorption.

01. Second floor: View of orchestra seating and control room. The seat cushions, filled with a gel, are developed and manufactured by Royal Medica, an Italian company specializing in ergonomically engineered pads and supports.

02. - 03. View into public gallery underneath seating wedge, with access to bathrooms.

04. Ground floor: ticketing booth is housed within the old bank safe.

05. Exterior view across Eighth Avenue. The vertical bank windows are retained, opening the theater to the street.

06. Section looking north.

01.

02.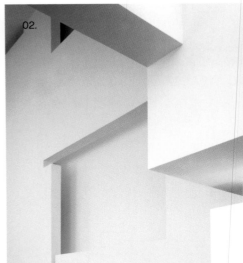

03.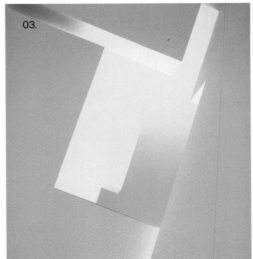

04.

D. E. Shaw & Company

120 West 45th Street
Steven Holl Architects
1992

D. E. Shaw & Co. is a small financial services company founded in 1988. The firm's operations are inextricably tied to the ebb and flow of global markets, monitored at all hours by a bank of tireless computers and servers. The design Steven Holl developed for this interior project is conceived as a parallel response to this unseen, abstract industry. The top two floors of a midtown skyscraper are the site of an experimental project exploring the phenomena of spatial color reflection, what Holl calls "projected color."

The office is gathered around a 31-foot reception hall. Mounted on steel studs, the gypsum-board walls are incised at precise points to form shadow boxes. Pigment has been applied to the back or bottom surfaces of these perforations, invisible to the viewer looking up from the lobby. Natural and artificial lights project this color back. The intensity of the colors being reflected is adjusted by a range of fluorescent tints. At night, these surfaces are backlit by a row of concealed lamps and transform the upper stories of the tower into a beacon.

01. The double-height reception space.

02. - 03. Invisible to the viewer, paint applied behind these cutouts are projected back into the reception hall.

04. The adjoining conference table is fashioned out of riveted steel panels, and shallow cutouts reveal CTR monitors in a playful adaptation of the wall details in the main room. Custom lamps diffusing incandescent light are suspended from the ceiling.

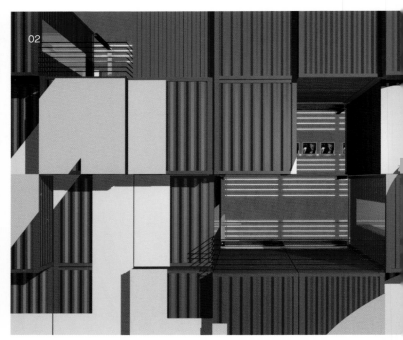

C-Mall

42nd Street and Fifth Avenue
Lot/ek
Design Completed 2003

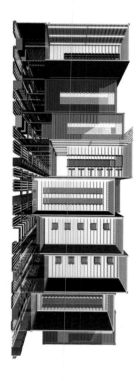

06.

This mixed-use retail and entertainment complex is proposed for the northeast corner of 42nd Street and Fifth Avenue, at the mid-point of Times Square and Grand Central Station. Dubbed C-Mall, it is a gridded, vertical elaboration on the sprawling mass of red shipping containers Lot/ek designed for the Gorée Museum and Memorial in Dakar, (1997).

On a site previously reserved by the developer LCOR for a crystalline Kohn Pedersen Fox skyscraper, and diagonally across the restored New York Public Library and Bryant Park, the low-rise C-Mall scheme stacks over a hundred containers on top of an L-shaped footprint. Reaching a height of nine stories, the facade mimics the extended shelves of a card catalog, its individual elements jockeying for position along the length of the sidewalk.

With the circulation core set against the back wall, the program envisaged for the corrugated assemblage includes a generous retail program, food courts and a variety of interactive play spaces for children of all ages, including a rock-climbing wall. Glazed perforations and protected balconies overlook the street, breaking up the monolithic street wall and affording passersby views of the activities within.

01. - 02. Exterior views along 42nd Street.

03. - 04. Corridor views.

05. Elevation along Fifth Avenue detailing the circulation core along the wall of the adjacent building to the north.

06. Section looking east.

THE
PYLONS
AT THE
CHRYSLER
CENTER

RETAIL
OWROOM
SPACE
AILABLE

Chrysler Center Trylons

155 East 42nd Street
Philip Johnson / Alan Ritchie Architects
2001

Rising mid-block, these three interlocking glass-and-steel structures form part of the $100 million Chrysler Center project. Together with the granite boxes that flank them, the three-sided "trylons" are part of a 22,000-square-foot retail pavilion that offers a programmatic connection between the Chrysler Building and Chrysler East—the former Kent Building—at 666 Third Avenue.

The crystalline pyramids rise to heights ranging between 60 and 70 feet. A framework of tubular steel supports more than 500 custom-sized glass panes. The materials and steep angles are meant to evoke the Chrysler Building's chevron windows and stainless-steel spire a thousand feet overhead. A low-rising fountain spans the base of the pyramids along 42nd Street.

Originally intended to house a restaurant, the interior space is being recast by its developers as a flagship location for an upmarket retail tenant. It is currently vacant.

The project also includes an exterior recladding and lobby renovation for Chrysler East. New mullions and wall panels emphasize vertical movement, and a bay extension adds floor-to-ceiling glass windows and views to the formerly blank western facade while creating 146,000 square-feet of new office space. Steel-clad columns prop up the lobby, which extends into a corridor leading to the adjacent retail space.

01. Principal street elevation.

International Center of Photography

1133 Avenue of the Americas
Gwathmey Siegel Architects
2001

Founded in 1974, the International Center of Photography (ICP) occupied an historic Georgian townhouse on Fifth Avenue's Museum Mile at 94th Street. The museum expanded to a satellite midtown facility in 1989, but by the late 1990s had outgrown its headquarters building. In 2000, the ICP undertook a major renovation of its midtown location, a 24,000 square-foot ground and and lower-level space at the base of an existing Manhattan office building. This redesign provides adaptable galleries for photography and new media exhibitions within a contemporary museum environment.

A transparent street-level entry leads into the reception lobby and adjacent museum store. Beyond the lobby, the visitor proceeds through a series of flexible initial galleries that progress toward an open, double-height stair leading to the lower level, which contains additional galleries, a cafe, and support space.

The descent allows visitors to experience the museum's full vertical volume, which is further emphasized by a single stainless-steel column that extends through both levels and an iconic ceiling skylight. Recessed lighting and frosted glass illuminate the exhibition space, while wood floors and stainless steel materials provide simple counterpoints to the white interior walls.

Located across the street from the ICP's school facility, the gallery helps establish a new urban campus for the institution. The museum more than doubles the previous exhibition space and becomes the new headquarters for the museum's public exhibitions programs.

01. Interior view looking out to entry.

02. Interior view of ground floor and basement level galleries.

02.

01.

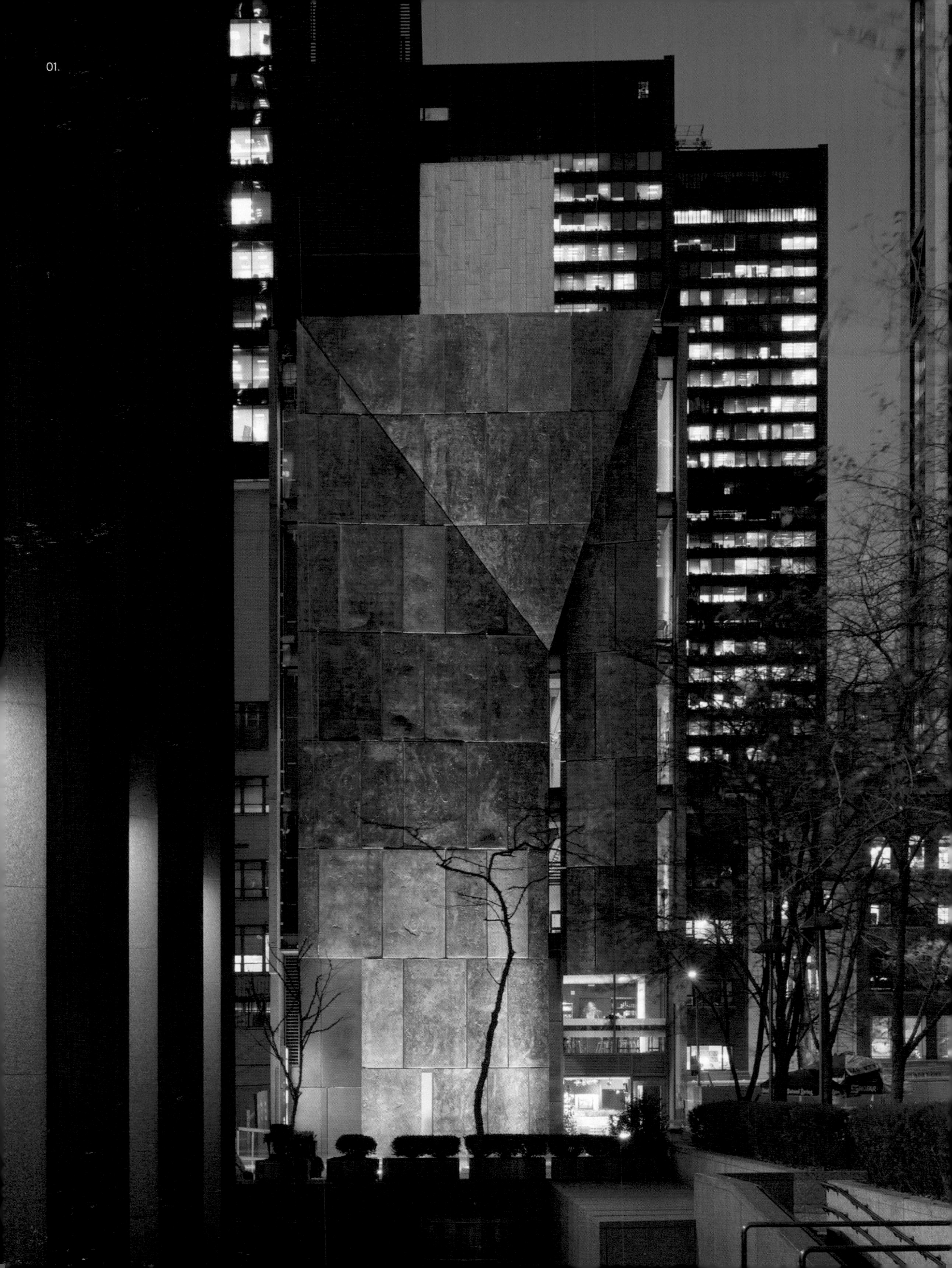

American Folk Art Museum

45 West 53rd Street
Tod Williams Billie Tsien Architects
2001

02.

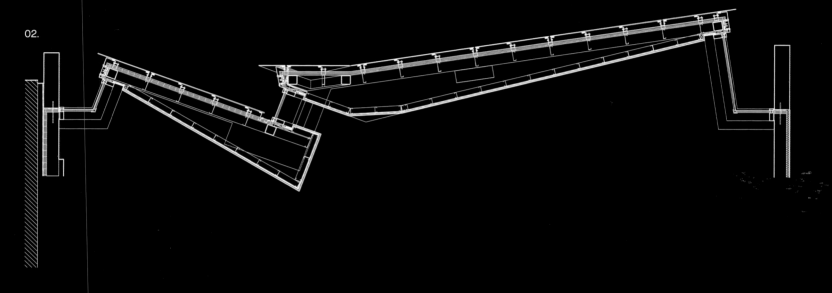

This eight-story building is the permanent home of the American Folk Art Museum (AFAM), an institution that previously occupied a number of smaller sites in Manhattan. With an area of 30,000 square-feet, the new structure is four times the size of the Eva & Morris Feld Gallery on Columbus and 65th Street, an exhibition space that the museum still maintains. The new AFAM is flanked by properties belonging to the Museum of Modern Art, and its principal elevation—facing south on 53rd Street—was conceived in part as a formal response to its much larger neighbor. Referencing the human hand, the built gesture is sculptural, like a palm creased to form a gently faceted wall. Tombasil—a type of white bronze—was cast through provisional molds on the floor of a foundry to create the metallic skin. Sectioned like armored plate, tolerances between each bronze panel reveal the black wall of the weather barrier behind it. Like a prism, it refracts natural and projected light into a broad spectrum of moods.

The four upper floors house the permanent and temporary exhibitions. Sunlight enters the galleries and filters down the building through a skylight above a grand staircase on the third floor. The museum's collection is showcased through a combination of traditional and non-traditional displays. The architects describe an exhibition program whereby art is "integrated into public spaces, utilizing a series of niches throughout the building that offer informal interaction with a changing series of folk art objects. The experience of the museum visitor is an architectural journey, encouraging often surprising encounters with both new and familiar objects by using multiple and sometimes redundant paths of circulation."

The mezzanine level, with a view out to 53rd Street, hosts a small cafe with a privileged view of the main hallway and the two-story atrium. The building extends two levels below grade: one floor contains the new auditorium and classrooms; the lowest level incorporates administrative offices, a library and an archive. At grade is a museum store, accessible during non-museum hours through an independent entrance.

01. View looking north of white-bronze facade.

02. Third floor plan, detail.

Cullman/Danziger Family Atrium

09. View looking north, second-floor galleries.

10. Third floor: View of nine-foot *Chief Tamanny Weathervane* (1890).

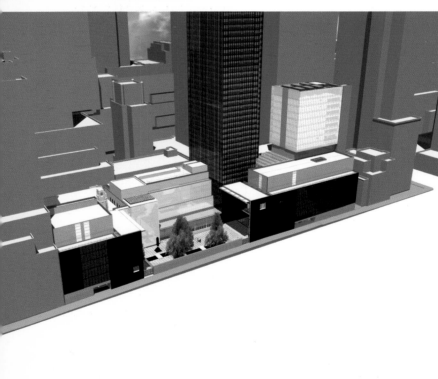

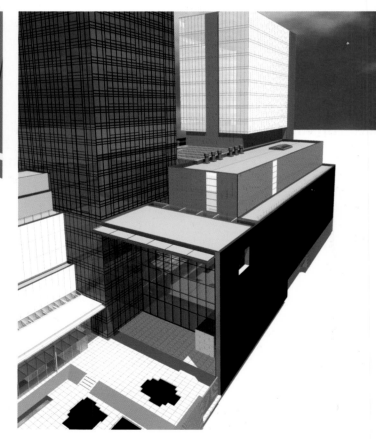

MoMA

11 West 53rd Street
Yoshio Taniguchi
2005 Completion

Beginning with the purchase of a modest townhouse off Fifth Avenue in 1932, the trustees of the Museum of Modern Art have bought piecemeal virtually all the surrounding plots on West 53rd Street, in their mission to create a suitably grand showplace for twentieth-century art in midtown Manhattan. This gradual process of collecting real estate encouraged a fitful building program that spanned over half a century. Its major phases— in 1939, 1951, 1953, 1964, 1980, and 1984— produced a number of important architectural contributions to the urban fabric. But the ever-expanding facility never quite kept pace with a collection that grew out of an inaugural gift of eight prints and a drawing, into one that currently includes over 100,000 paintings, sculptures and other art objects.

In 1997, MoMA called for a comprehensive architectural solution that significantly increases the area dedicated to exhibitions and related programs, addresses a demonstrated need for natural light, and improves building circulation. After a much-publicized international charette involving ten firms, the Tokyo-based architect Yoshio Taniguchi was selected out of three finalists in 1998. Known

chiefly for designing a number of minimalist repositories for Japanese art and ethnographic artifacts, like the Horyu-ji Gallery in Ueno Park (1999), the new MoMA is Taniguchi's first North American commission.

All told, Taniguchi's scheme (with Kohn Pedersen Fox as executive architect) will feature 630,000 square-feet of new and redesigned space to meet the museum's requirements for the twenty-first century. The design concentrates the larger volumes of space devoted to the galleries in the western portion of the site, while the spaces devoted to education and research are located in the eastern portion. From 54th Street, the two volumes are intended to make the Museum's mission explicit: "The two simple geometric forms, one accommodating the galleries and the other educational facilities, symbolize the dual mission of the museum."

Taniguchi's original proposal identifies the Abby Aldrich Rockefeller Sculpture Garden (1953) as the principal exterior element. The southern terrace, which was part of Philip Johnson's original design for the garden, is reestablished, thereby restoring the diagonal

01. - 04. Views along 54th Street showing the position of the expanded Abby Aldrich Rockefeller Sculpture Garden and the new exhibition wing to the west of the site.

05. Site plan. The block is bordered to the north by 54th Street, to the south by 53rd Street, and to the west by Sixth Avenue.

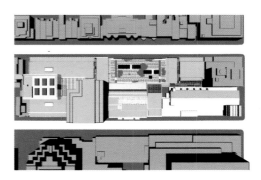

05.

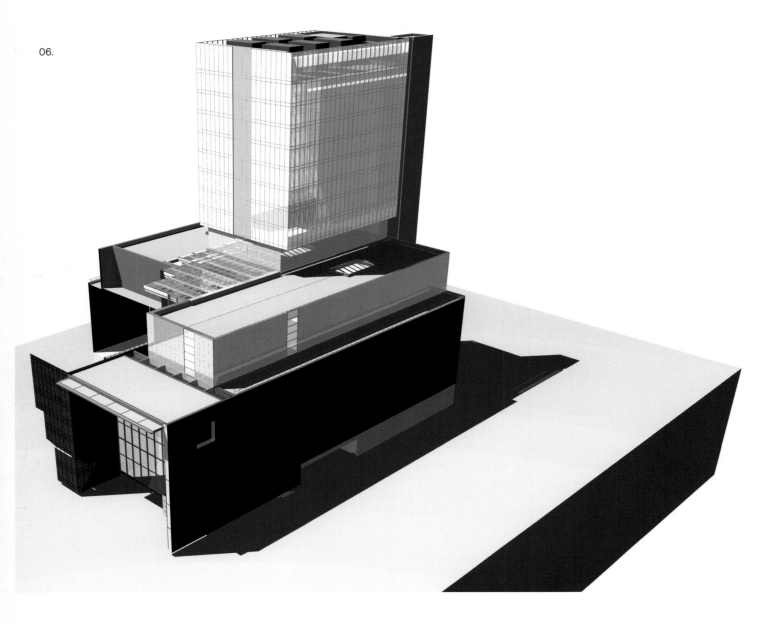

relationship between its principal components that was lost in subsequent alterations. While the plan of the garden regains its original integrity, the proposal does not seek merely to return it to its original appearance. The open space of the garden is broadened to the east, west and south.

The Museum's midtown Manhattan context figures prominently in a number of design decisions. A through-block entry from 53rd to 54th Streets is set up—with the principal entry on the latter street—recalling a number of recent mid-block interventions nearby. Taniguchi addresses the verticality of the public spaces integral to the architectural culture of midtown with an asymmetrical atrium that underscores this vertical organization in the interior of the Museum, while the atrium's placement reveals the northeast corner of Cesar Pelli's Museum Tower (1984).

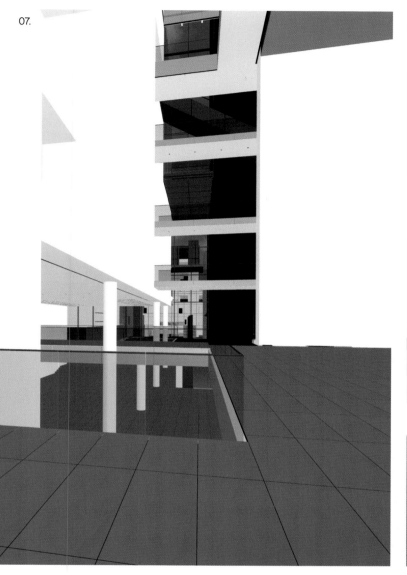

07.

08.

09.

06. A new gallery building on the western portion of the site will house the main exhibition galleries. The Museum's first stand-alone Education and Research Center on the eastern portion of the site will provide over five times more space for classrooms, auditoriums, teacher training workshops, and the Museum's expanded Library and Archives. These two buildings will frame the enlarged Abby Aldrich Rockefeller Sculpture Garden.

07. - 09. Interior views under the main skylight of the new gallery building. The architect proposed that the earliest works in the collections be situated in the upper Collection Galleries rather than in the lower spaces. The intention is not necessarily to reverse the visitor's experience of the collection but, rather, to take advantage of the fact that each floor can be considered a specific destination, and that the lower, larger floors are more suited to contemporary works.

Austrian Cultural Forum

11 East 52nd Street
Atelier Raimund Abraham
2001

The concept for this landmark tower, by the Austrian-born architect Raimund Abraham, bested the proposals of 225 other entrants in an international design competition held in 1992. Abraham handed the construction documents to the client, the Austrian Ministry of Foreign Affairs, two years later, but it would be another seven lean years before the scheme was realized. The heightened sense of anticipation—at least among architects, and not least to the consular functionaries it was intended to house—appears to have been very well placed.

In designing the American nexus of Austria's cultural outreach, Abraham, who taught at the Cooper Union for a quarter of a century, has presented midtown with a curious, and even menacing, architectural puzzle. Formally, it is less like the mask and vertebrae the architect describes in his competition brief, but more like a siege tower. Breaking out of the street wall, the twenty-story building cascades onto the pavement, an interrupted shower of aggregate, glass and steel. Four sloping glass plates—shingled like lamellar armor— rake outward from the steep wedge. A third of the way up the facade, a concrete box

resembling a battlement with narrow defensive slits is suspended from one of the glass eaves. (This aerie is actually the director's office). Structural details visible from the interior, especially the zones directly behind the expanse of glass looking out across the street elicit a power that belies its transparent delicacy.

The institute's 25,000 square-feet is crammed into a plot measuring 80-feet-wide and only 25-feet-deep. Which isn't to say that the building is spatially or operationally inconsistent with its mission to promote culture: the placement of vertical circulation to the rear of the site allowed for the narrow street frontage to be maximized. The structure generously accommodates the mostly educational and office program. Above grade, the functions include a library, a double-height, 80-seat theater, conference and seminar spaces, and administrative offices. The basement cradles a small art gallery.

01. View along street wall looking east.

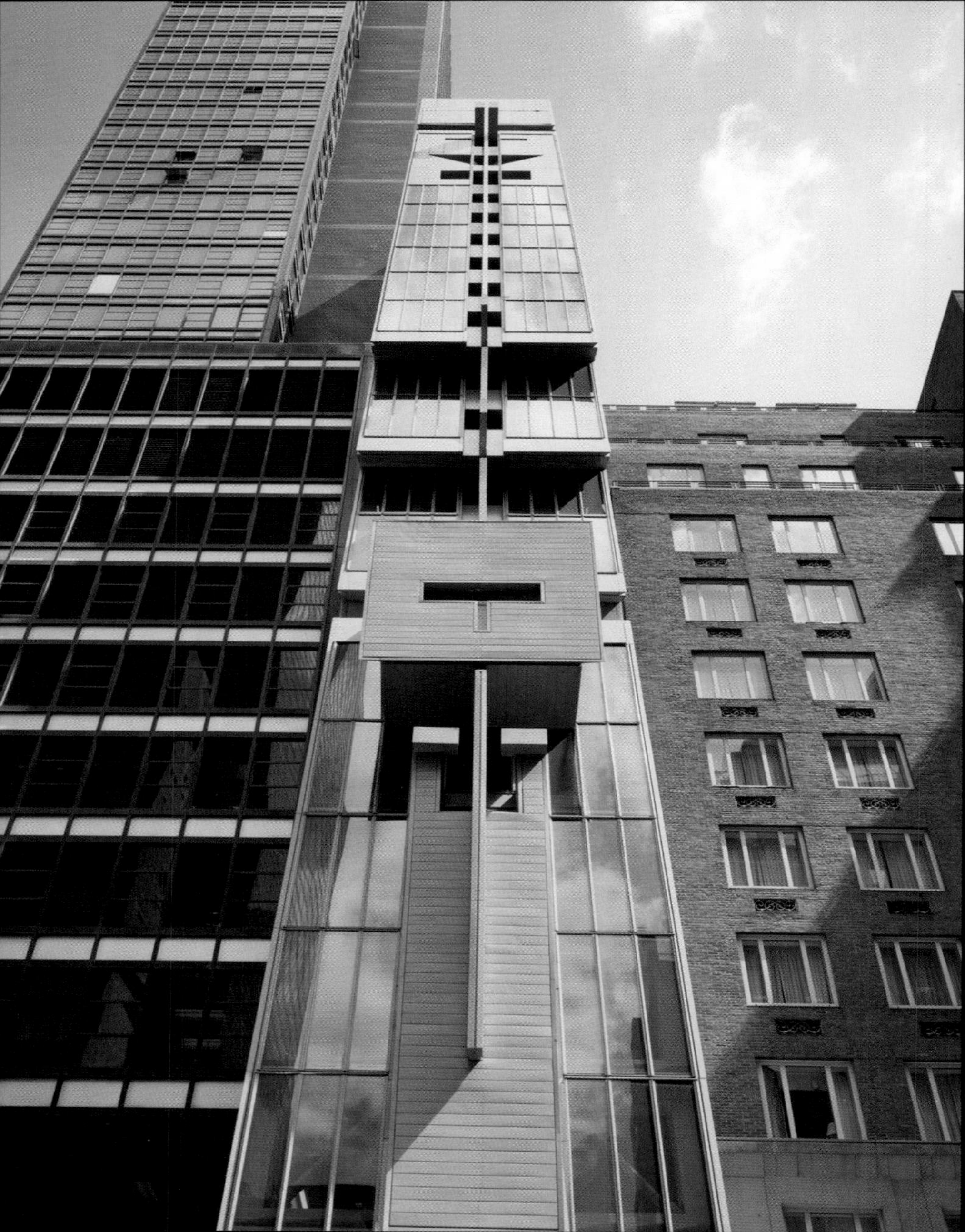

Brasserie

100 East 53rd Street
Diller + Scofidio
2000

For their first construction in Manhattan, Diller + Scofidio instigated the transformation of the noted French brasserie—gutted by fire in 1995—in the cellar of Mies van der Rohe's Seagram building. The new interior uses skins of wood, terrazzo, tile, and glass that lift away from their surfaces to become structural, spatial and functional elements.

In the main dining area, a madrone floor peels up to meet the cascading pear wood ceiling panel halfway, and the resulting banquette becomes part of a continuous wrapper around the space. Wood skins in the rear dining room break off from the ceiling and wall to form free-floating partitions.

Despite being housed within an iconic Modernist tower, the restaurant is entirely without glass or view, and the design plays on this irony. Glass straddles a stone wall at the entry, and a video camera provides time-elapsed views of the street via plasma monitors inside. A sensor in the restaurant's revolving door triggers each snapshot, announcing every new arrival on the ever-changing LCD display over the bar. A staircase prolongs the descent of patrons into the main dining room, putting them on display.

A series of tall, upholstered slabs, set at an angle and propped on steel legs, slice the slender space flanking the dining area. Poured resin dining tables are formed around stainless-steel structural supports that remain visible through the material. At the bar, steel tripods support seats injected with medical gel.

Hexagonal tiles and opalescent honeycomb panels provide a visual connection between the separate men's and women's bathrooms, which share a cast resin sink that spans both spaces and empties into a single drain.

01. The bar is positioned along the west wall. Monitors above it project time-elapsed photographs of entering patrons.

03.

02. View of the main dining room looking north to the entry stair.

03. The booths along the east wall reference the 1958 original by Philip Johnson.

08.

04. - 05. The continuous glass wall along the rear
dining room is a shadow box featuring a
series of custom sculptures.

Each glass plate is actually composed of
two panes with a special film sandwiched in
between to create optical effects.

06. - 07. The separate men's and women's
bathrooms share a cast resin sink that
empties into a single drain.

08. In the main dining area, a madrone floor peels
up to meet the cascading pear wood ceiling
panel halfway to form a banquette.

Chambers & Town

15 West 56th Street
Rockwell Group
Adams Soffes Wood
2001

Built in the twilight of New York's boutique hotel explosion, the 77-room Chambers Hotel is situated on 56th Street, between Fifth and Sixth avenues. Financed by the consortium partly responsible for Christian Liaigre's Mercer Hotel (1999), the clients appointed pop instigator David Rockwell and Lawrence Adams of Adams Soffes Wood to whip up a fifteen-story structure out of a mid-block parking garage flanked by Norma Kamali, Fendi and Felissimo. Facing south, the facade is set back in a typical wedding-cake section and clad in smooth limestone.

Ushered through a pair of massive lattice-work doors of black walnut, guests enter a two-story lobby littered with artwork and an eclectic mix of furniture. The architects describe a concept intended to "create an intimate, residential feeling, as if stepping into the townhouse of a private art collector." Artists' lofts are referenced as models for the guest rooms and suites, all of which are adorned with original works of art.

The corridors along the guest room floors display the work of a dozen artists (and at least one flamboyant auteur). Most of the site-specific pieces take the form of murals and are part of a curated program developed by the architects, the art consultancy Museum Editions and participating galleries, and include installations by Bob and Roberta Smith, Do-Ho Suh, John Newsom, Katharina Grosse, Alyson Shotz, and John Waters.

Beaded and covered in a backlit grid of sueded, square panels, the main dining hall of the Chambers' set-piece restaurant, Town —operated by chef Geoffrey Zakarian of Patroon and 44—evokes a sense of lightness despite its subterranean setting. Prefaced by a bar and accessed through a stair descending from a cantilevered lounge on the first floor, the double-height room soars to a height of 24 feet. Designed to accommodate a hundred patrons, this central space is cast in neutral colors. A sequence of 6-foot high blond wood screens surround the banquettes and the freestanding tables, while a scrim of small laminated mirrors suspended from floor-height wire cables line the core wall of both main dining room and lounge, lending an extra measure of glitter.

01. Detail, black walnut doors.

02. Entrance view looking into lobby.

03. Chambers: view of double-height lobby.

04. Chambers: detail of guest room door on the fourth floor, with mural by Bob and Roberta Smith.

05. Town: a curving banquette looks into the main dinning area below.

01.

Christian Dior

LVMH

21 East 57th Street
Atelier Christian de Portzamparc
1999

02.   03.   04.   05.

Incorporated in 1987, the Louis Vuitton–Moët Hennessy group shepherds a diverse list of luxury brands, ranging from a core group of fashion houses, jewelers and vintners to duty-free shop operators and art auctioneers. Based in Paris, LVMH selected a site along a row of shops on the north side of 57th Street between Fifth and Madison Avenues as the headquarters of its North American operations.

The 93,500-square-foot building occupies a narrow footprint measuring 60-by-100-feet. It would have assumed the conventional form of a single, stepped block had the scheme rigidly adhered to prescribed limits on height and volume. The building code permitted a certain percentage of volume on the aligned facades, so the architects devised a novel interpretation of the setback regulations to highlight the formal and material presence of the 24-story tower. Initially, the Wally Findlay

Gallery was to have remained intact at the foot of the building, cramping the site. The early responses to the constraints placed by this problem were a number of intermediate schemes. Following the purchase of the lot in its entirety, the project matured into its present form.

The final design is dominated by a bold, faceted shell cleverly masking what is essentially a stepped parti. Just above the Christian Dior boutique occupying the base of the tower, the glass-and-steel curtainwall divides into asymmetrical halves. Simulating a subduction zone, one sharp edge slips below the edge of the other for the first ten stories. On the eleventh floor, the building gently steps—sways—back, and one of the plates tapers to a knifepoint at the crown. The walls are of clear glass, some fritted to an opalescent white, and low-emissivity

green glass. The three-part facade acquires prismatic qualities at night, when it is animated by a multicolored array of fiber optics embedded underneath its translucent skin.

The slight proportions of the tower have led to relatively compact working conditions, considering the number of companies that now operate within it. But users contend that the premium of space on the office floors is offset by the double-height "magic room" at the top of the tower, a dedicated party space commanding views of the city, replete with a grand staircase. Partygoers alighting from the elevator descend from the top of the stair to reach the event floor.

Preceding pages:

06. - 09. Views along 57th street.

10. Northwest corner, 57th Street and Madison Avenue. Edward Larrabee Barnes' IBM Tower (1983) stands with Alexander Calder's *Saurien* (1975), on the southwest corner.

11. Upper level conference room.

12. View looking west above 57th street, from the double-height "magic room" on the 23rd floor.

13. - 14. Views through the distinctive clear and translucent glass utilized on the curtainwall from inside and out.

11.

12.

13.

14.

01. View looking west. By peeling away the corners at the diagonals, the vertical proportions of the tower are emphasized, along with a distinctively faceted silhouette. From the inside, this device creates spaces that will feature panoramic views of Central Park and the Hudson River.

02. View looking south.

03. Tower section, looking west.

04. AOL/Time Warner Building, by Skidmore, Owings & Merrill (2004). View looking south.

Hearst Tower

959 Eighth Avenue
Foster and Partners
Design Completed 2001

02.

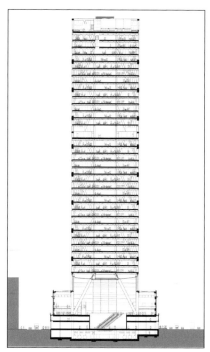

03.

04.

In the 1920s, William Randolph Hearst commissioned the Viennese émigré Joseph Urban to design the first phase of a twenty-story tower on the southwest corner of 57th Street and Eighth Avenue. The International News Building was to be the centerpiece of a new entertainment district just south of Columbus Circle. But by 1928, only the podium—a six-story Art Deco masonry block, with splayed corners, allegorical statuary, and columns that project one floor above the roof—was completed. With the onset of the Great Depression, plans to cap the base with a tower were abandoned.

It would be seven decades—excepting an abortive attempt in the 1980s—before executives at the Hearst Corporation reconsidered the project. The current rationale, to consolidate the disparate editorial and business offices of the seventeen glossies published by the company into one corporate edifice, was a move no doubt spurred by a similar strategy at Condé Nast Magazines which moved to Fox and Fowle's Four Times Square in 1999, and certainly made more urgent by the selection of the final schemes for the New York Times tower and the Columbus Circle Competition.

Hearst selected a veteran of the New York Times competition, the London-based Foster and Partners, to graft nearly one million square-feet of new program to the existing building. The firm was chosen in no small measure for its work with historic structures—which include the recently completed interventions for the Reichstag and the British Museum—as much for their signature skyscrapers in Europe and Asia. The new structure is lifted clear off the landmark base, linked on the outside by columns and glazing, which are set back from the edges of the site.

The transparent connection illuminates the spaces below with natural light, spatially and experientially distinguishing old and new. Escalators take visitors to a large landscaped atrium with cafés, restaurants and exhibition areas.

The new Hearst tower will have an efficient triangulated structure similar to that employed in Foster's Commerzbank in Frankfurt. Expressed on the exterior in stainless-steel, the configuration offers more structural redundancy than a conventional grid of vertical columns and horizontal beams. In consultation with the city's Landmarks Preservation Commission, Sir Norman Foster describes their approach as "combining the best of both worlds—the old and the new—to enhance the historic through a careful dialogue with the modern."

356 West 58th Street
Philippe Starck
2000

In 1984, Ian Schrager and Steve Rubell called on Andrée Putman to whip up a 113-room hotel on Madison Avenue and 37th Street, one block north of the Morgan Library. Blending the scale of Old World inns with the amenities of a modern luxury hotel, Morgans is often credited with spawning the dominant trend in contemporary hostelry. For a follow-up, Schrager enlisted the services of a fellow provocateur, the Parisian architect Philippe Starck, to convert a onetime bachelor's residence off Fifth Avenue and 44th Street into the 205-room Royalton (1989). Starck's flair for the theatrical hastened the evolution of the type into pure spectacle, and with Schrager's consistent patronage, he exported the boutique concept far and abroad throughout the 1990s.

Under the shadow of AOL/Timer Warner's twin towers, Starck's Hudson hotel stands at the southeast corner of 58th Street and Ninth Avenue. Opened in October 2000, the 26-story building it occupies first served as the American Women's Association clubhouse in 1928. It became the first Hudson Hotel in the 1930s, and was most recently a production and administrative facility for WNET TV 13 before Schrager and his partners acquired the property.

A flat, building-wide expanse of stucco, and planters for mock poplars mark the facade at street level. A solitary doorway funnels guests to an escalator—framed by a proscenium of clear and sandblasted glass, and bathed in chartreuse floodlights—that leads up to a 40-foot high lobby on the second floor. Descended from the Morgans and the Royalton, but at one thousand guestrooms—roughly 420,000 square-feet—the Hudson certainly qualifies as a boutique hotel, although a very large one. Its operational model is really the 600-room Paramount in Times Square (1990), also by Starck.

Much of the hotel's flash is really derived from the party spaces on the upper floors, which include an outdoor garden, and several lounges. Opposite the check-in counter on the second floor, the Hudson Bar is the main draw. The bar is a set-piece extravaganza, replete with a glass-block floor, a brick fireplace, club chairs, deer antler lamps, and a Francesco Clemente ceiling. Starck's Catskills-meets-Manhattan baroque gibes noisily with the minimalism of the entry sequence, and it is precisely through these kinds of juxtapositions that Starck produces drama worthy of the hype.

01. The Hudson: 58th Street facade.

02. The Royalton: 44th Street entry.

02.

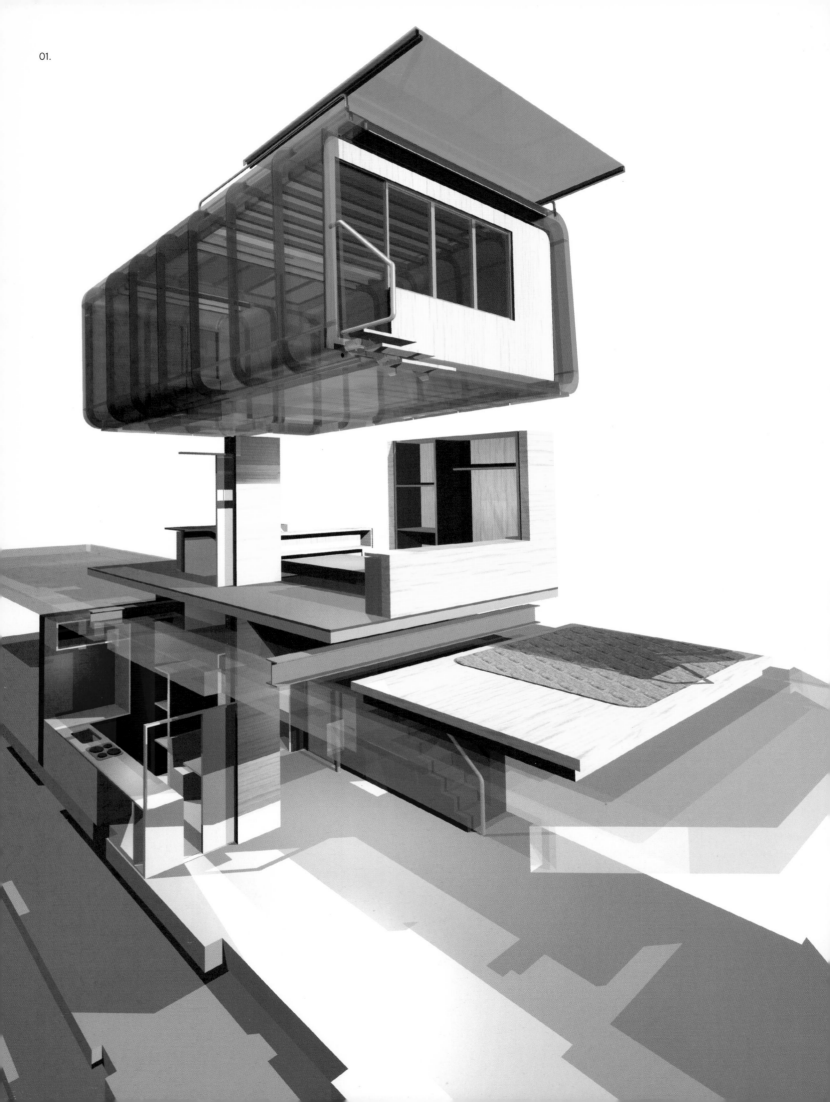

Jellyfish Rooftop Housing

46 West 71st Street
SU 11
Design Completed 2002

02.

Ferda Kolatan and Erich Schoenenberger of SU 11 conceived this rooftop extension and renovation of an existing apartment on the Upper West Side as a "habitable puzzle." Measuring a total area of 1,000 square-feet, the components of this puzzle are several spatial and functional "units" consisting of object, furniture and space.

These set-piece units are programmatically sequenced to form a hybrid but irreducible assemblage. The compound nature of each unit is underscored by the fact that some of its constituent parts are new and others are preexisting. The color and material coding of the units—red, orange, wood—are not merely diagrammatic but are actually applied to the materials.

The gap separating the existing building envelope containing the main floor of the apartment and the new penthouse addition floating above the rooftop surface is characterized by the architects as a "temporal (before/after) and spatial (inside/outside)" link between the two halves. The location of the horizontal openings (stair shaft, rooftop skylight) and vertical openings (windows, doors) permit the space to extend further.

Incorporating the bedroom, the "jellyfish" penthouse acts as a membrane protecting the interior "organs" of living and working below. A structurally independent unit on its own, it is simply placed on steel beams over the surface of the building like the water tanks, air conditioners and aerials that litter Manhattan roofscapes. The simplicity of its geometry and the nature of its detached state to the rooftop allow for prefabricated sections of various sizes and features to be delivered on site and installed in place.

01. Exploded axonometric rendering.

02. Section looking west.

03. View looking southwest towards Lincoln Center and ABC/Capital Cities complex.

03.

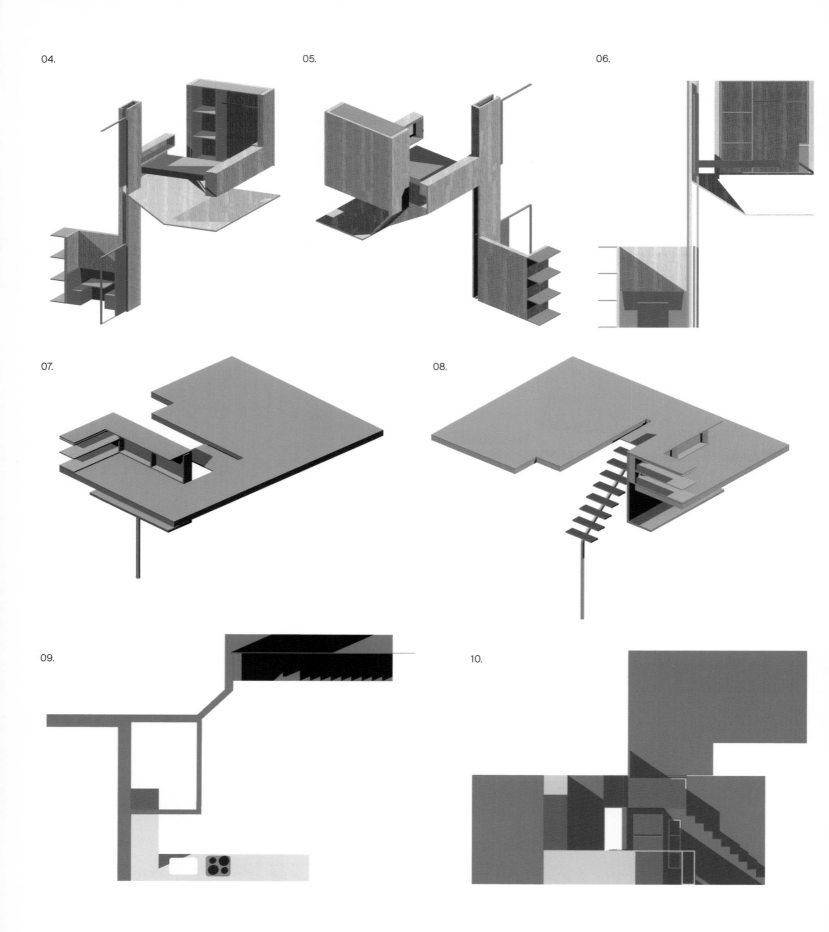

04. **05.** **06.**

07. **08.**

09. **10.**

04. - 15. The color and material coding of the individual units making up the apartment—red, orange, wood—are not merely diagrammatic but are actually applied to materials themselves.

238

11.

12.

13.

14.

15.

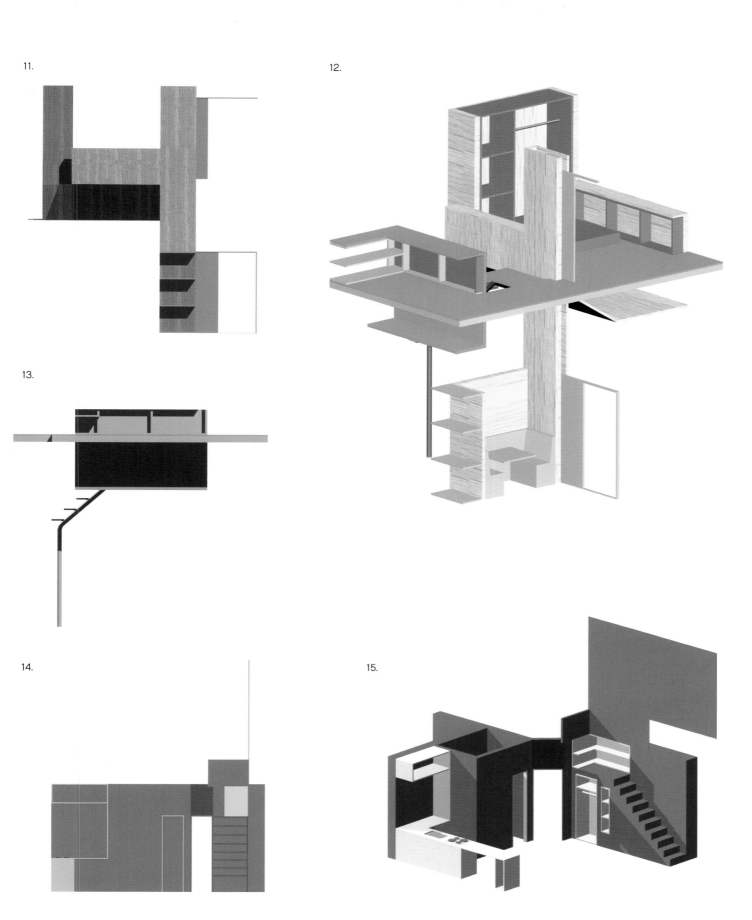

72nd Street Townhouse

176 East 72nd Street
Tod Williams Billie Tsien Architects
1996

This 15,000-square-foot single-family house occupies the footprint of two demolished brownstones on East 72nd Street, between Lexington and Third avenues. Nestled between a five-story consulate and an eighteen-story apartment building, the six-story building cuts a singular presence on the south side of this wide, crosstown street, as it connects to its neighbors in materials and scale. Designed by the New York firm of Tod Williams and Billie Tsien, it is one of a relatively small number of townhouses built from the ground up in the last twenty years, attesting to the viability and enduring appeal of the type.

The central feature of the facade is a hammered limestone wall enclosed within an arch of fritted and transparent glass. The wall affords the residents a sense of protection and privacy from the busy street. The arrangement of the windows surrounding the stone filters sunlight into the rooms. The rear of the building, facing a 30-foot-by-30-foot garden, is predominantly glazed and compositionally related to the treatment of the street elevation. A large skylight crowns the building. Flooding the interiors in natural light, it encourages vertical circulation by illuminating a stairway that runs from the basement level to the top floor. Defining the sense of movement is a monumental wall, one echoing the limestone exterior.

The building section places each of the major program areas in the most logical and effective location, with a pool in the basement; family, kitchen and dining on the ground floor; and living, study and library on the second (double-height) floor. The guest room is on a mezzanine level, parents and child's room on the third level, and staff rooms on the top floor.

01. View along 72nd Street looking west. Floors in public areas are kirkstone and cherry. Cabinetwork is cherry. All interiors, including furniture and carpets, were custom-designed by the architects

02. Second floor: View looking up skylight.

03. The double-height living room viewed from
the third floor.

04. Interior view. Second-floor living room
    looking north.

05. North elevation with views of the ground-floor
    garden and major program areas.

Rose Center for Earth and Space

81st Street and Central Park West
Polshek Partnership
2000

This project is one of several architectural interventions undertaken by the American Museum of Natural History in the 1990s to reshape the image of the 130-year-old institution for a new generation of visitors. All told, the new Frederick Phineas & Sandra Priest Rose Center for Earth and Space incorporates some 333,500 square-feet of new construction—the equivalent of a major museum on its own. Built to replace the outdated (but landmarked) Hayden Planetarium built in 1935, it increases the total square footage of the museum by twenty-five percent.

The exhibition program is contained within the largest suspended glass curtain wall in North America. An acre of glass—in 736 individual panes—was used to construct the 95-foot-high enclosure. Entirely tension supported, the glass hangs from the roof of the facility, anchored by 1,400 steel "spiders," 4,100 bolts and approximately 2.5 miles of rod rigging. The 90-foot sphere encased within this glass cube ruled out traditional columnar

supports, and in its place are two-way roof trusses and a system of triangular wall trusses supporting its four walls.

Clad in perforated aluminum panels, the upper half of the Hayden Sphere houses a new planetarium and Zeiss star projector, while the lower portion is devoted to an interactive theater chronicling the 13-billion-year history of the universe. The sphere is linked to the ground by a spiraling ramp, connecting the sphere to Cullman Hall, a large exhibition area dominating the base of the cube. The sequence of exhibits at this level unites the Rose Center with the existing wings, linking astronomy with the other natural sciences.

Other project elements include a new Columbus Avenue entrance, expanded restaurant and retail facilities, an educational resource center, and parking beneath the landscaped Ross Terrace along 81st Street.

01. View looking east. The Hayden Sphere is clad in 2,474 fabricated aluminum panels containing 5,599,663 acoustic-enhancing perforations.

02. Section looking south from 81st Street.

03. Elevation along 81st Street.

04. Anchored by 4,100 bolts and approximately 2.5
miles of rod rigging, 736 panes of glass make
up the curtainwall. An average pane of glass is
5-by-10.5 feet and weighs 450 pounds.

05. View looking north to 81st Street from the ramp
connecting the base of the sphere to the
galleries below.

06. - 07. The new Zeiss projector inside the upper
half of the Hayden Sphere.

06.

07.

Duplex Apartment

Upper East Side
Maya Lin Studio
1998

The design of this Manhattan residence seeks to create a space intimate enough for a single person yet flexible enough to accommodate the client's family members and other visitors. Maya Lin envisioned "a home that could fold in on itself like origami or a Transformer toy, changing its shape or function depending on how it was used."

The entrance to the duplex is located at a midpoint between the lower-level public areas and upper-level bedrooms. The levels are visually separated by a narrow wood and steel wall that divides the wider staircase leading down to the public areas from the narrower staircase leading upstairs. An open entry area unifies the spaces and allows light to permeate the residence.

The adaptable top level consists of three bedrooms and two bathrooms. The two bathrooms, with their pivoting frosted glass shower and bath panels, can be combined into one, and a moveable wardrobe reconfigures two of the bedrooms into a single suite, with beds also designed for use as seating. The closet wall in the master bedroom conceals a workstation that can be hidden away completely when not in use.

Downstairs, a glass skylight runs the length of the living room, where a wall opens to reveal entertainment and office equipment. The kitchen island is designed as a puzzle, with drawers opening into cabinets and seating that folds away to form the back of the island. A buffet counter opens into a dining table and chairs.

01. View of fireplace from the stairs, which lead to the private spaces of the apartment. The downward stairway is wider, focusing attention onto the living room below.

02. View of stairs and kitchen from the living room.

03. The stairs behind the 2.5-inch-wide, wood-and-steel wall separating the intimate and the more public areas of the house.

04. The large bathroom at the top of the stairs can be divided into two smaller bathrooms by a sliding door.

01.

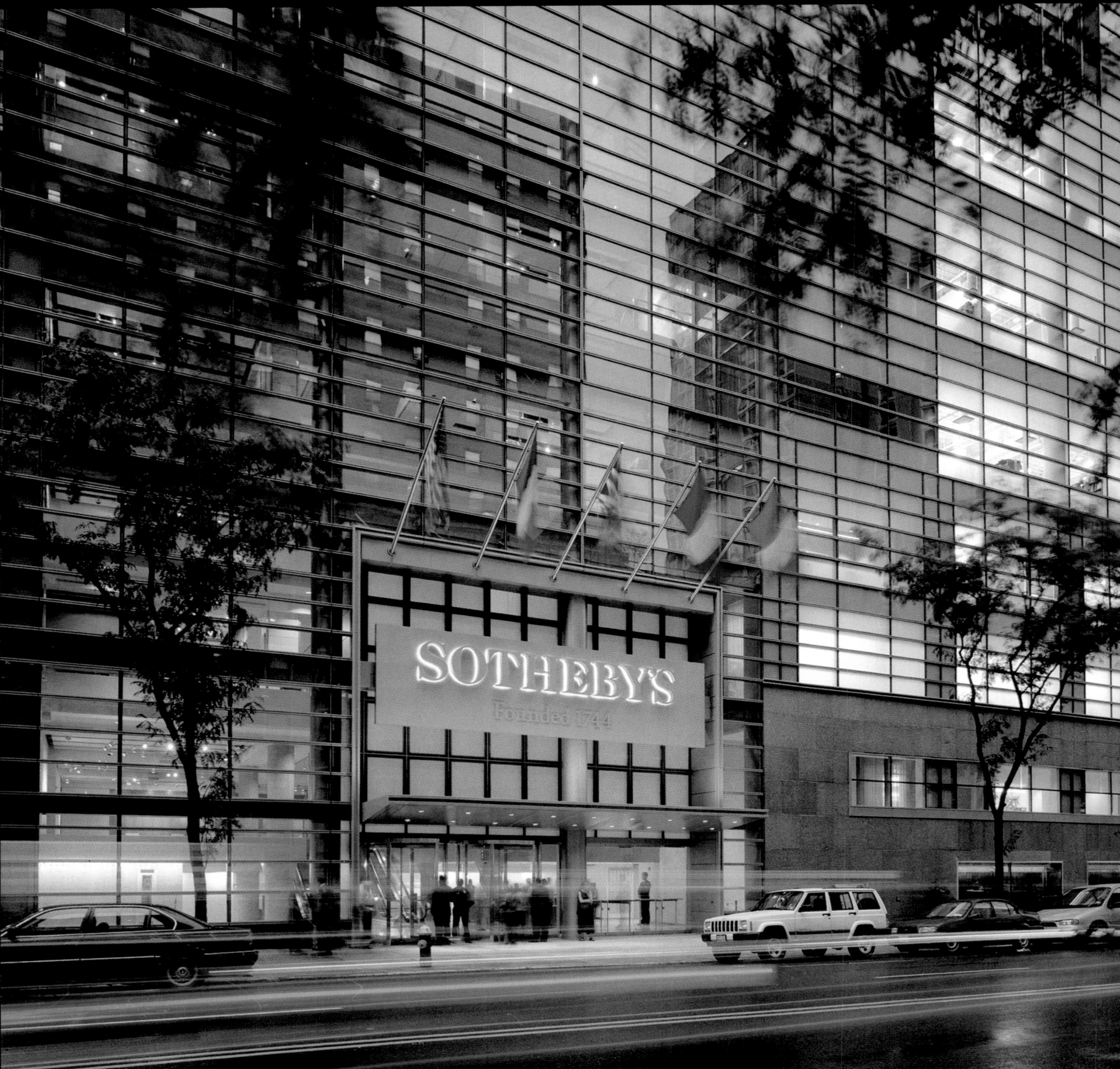

This project adapts Sotheby's granite-clad headquarters building on Manhattan's Upper East Side to meet the 255-year-old auction house's modern requirements. The resulting six-story addition incorporates the existing four-story structure as a podium while creating an entirely new identity for the building. Occupying a block-wide site on York Avenue and 71st Street, just north of New York-Cornell Medical Center and Rockefeller University, the building was constructed in the midst of a particularly troubled period in the history of Sotheby's North American operations.

A highly articulated glass curtainwall transmits generous amounts of natural light to the gallery spaces, providing an ideal environment for evaluating works of art. The changing wall module and mixture of transparent and translucent panels express the different functions on each floor. At night, the curtainwall becomes a signature design element, broadcasting the building's interior lighting to create a beacon visible throughout the mostly residential neighborhood.

Upon accessing the building from York Avenue, visitors enter a ten-story atrium in which hanging banners herald current displays and events. Central escalators rising from the main lobby provide access to public exhibition and sales areas, and an elevator cluster services all levels of the building.

The facility includes six floors of space for consignment storage, research, cataloging and exhibition areas for the various art and art object categories. The seventh floor houses the major auction sales room that can accommodate up to one thousand bidders and spectators. Administrative offices occupy floors eight and nine, and the top level includes a grand gallery for contemporary art and special collector sales. A cafe, teahouse and outdoor terrace and sculpture garden—all open to the public—complement the grand gallery spaces.

01. Northeast corner, 71st Street and York Avenue.

02. Principal facade on York Avenue displaying the different glazing types.

02.

03. The exhibition space designed by Richard Gluckman on the tenth floor.

04. Balcony overlooking the atrium.

05. Mezzanine level.

06. View looking up the nine-story atrium from ground level.

03.

04.

05.

01.

02.

Aida

209 East 76th Street
Archi-Tectonics
2000

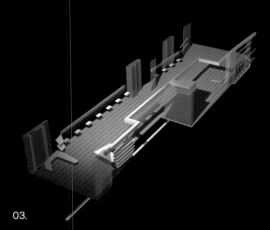

03.

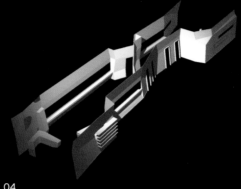

04.

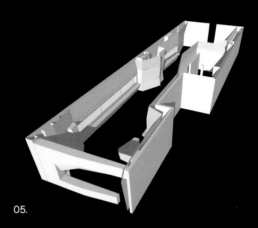

05.

The client enlisted Winka Dubbledam of Archi-Tectonics to fashion a hair salon out of a narrow 2,000-square-foot space on Manhattan's Upper East Side. With a mandate to attract a young clientele, the architect devised a solution that introduces a level of detail unusual for the type. Central to the scheme is a novel interior wall system conceived as a sculptural wrapper. Stretched over a tectonic frame, the walls themselves transform into functional elements, such as desks and seating elements, creating a fluid, unified space.

The facade consists of a dynamic bluestone wall that folds—and appears to float—over a single large pane of glass. This pane and the adjacent frameless glass door create an inviting transparent counterpoint to the density of the stone, allowing views and light deep into the salon and blurring the boundaries between interior and exterior.

The folded surfaces of the facade continue inside, where the angled white walls enclose integrated heating, cooling, and lighting systems, as well as sound equipment and floating mirrors. The walls fold out at intervals to provide additional private spaces. The sculptural void produced by this wrapper effect generates an organic space meant to resemble the human body.

Mirrors, chairs and hair-washing stations line the salon's interior walls, its leading edges dulled by soft lighting. The smooth wall surfaces extend into an enclosed courtyard, where a bamboo garden offers a relaxing place to wait during the warmer months.

01. Bluestone facade on 76th Street, between Third and Second avenues.

02. Reception area.

03. - 05. Axonometric renderings: Floor plan, wall system and envelope.

01.

01. The casement windows that form the spine of the elevation are operable.

02. The raised living and dining areas looking south, with views of fireplace and stair leading to the upper floors.

03. The second-floor main bathroom.

04. Day view. The children's room is on the half-level below grade.

525 East 85th Street

525 East 85th Street
Alexander Gorlin Architect
2003

Built in 1958, this modern townhouse on 85th Street, between York and East End avenues, was originally designed by architects John Brownrigg and Jean Paul Mitarachi for a prominent Manhattan couple. Formerly the Ekstrom Residence, an MTV executive recently bought the house, and its new owner required alterations to the existing structure to accommodate a growing family. The client appointed the New York practice of Alexander Gorlin to renovate and expand the existing structure.

Set back from the sidewalk by a 25-foot-deep garden, the townhouse is a composition of steel and glass distinct from its brick-faced neighbors. A facade of horizontal steel bands alternated with window walls defined the existing two-story construction, and apart from the elimination of a building-width balcony and the addition of a third floor, much of the building's original character has been

retained. The main floor is clad entirely in glass, in three large panes above smaller casement windows, revealing a vestibule and living room with a 12-foot-high ceiling. On the second and third stories, the glass curtain-wall is divided into smaller rectangular sections to create vertical movement.

The interior was gutted except for the main floor where the silver travertine floors and other original finishes were preserved. The stair was reconstructed and raised to the third level. A large skylight was introduced, bringing light down to the lower levels through a translucent floor composed of glass blocks. The children's playroom is set below grade, while the kitchen and dining areas adjoin the living room on the first floor. The main bedroom is located on the second floor, and the top floor consists of a guest room, an office and a media room that opens onto a terrace.

04.

01. Interior view along Fifth Avenue.

02. Perspective view looking south from Duke Ellington Memorial Ellipse.

03. Conceptual section looking east.

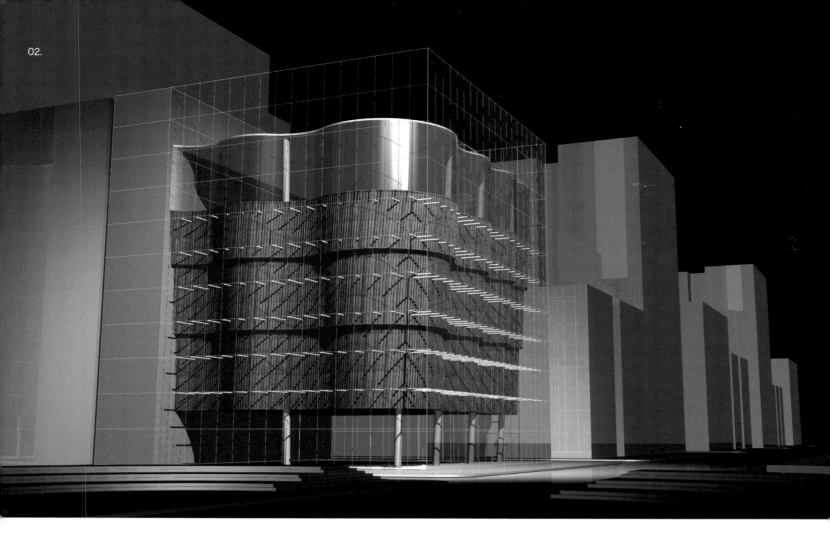

Museum for African Art

109-110th Street and Fifth Avenue
Bernard Tschumi Architects
Design Completed 1999

In 1999, the Museum for African Art (MAA) vacated its address on Broadway and Prince Street (designed by Maya Lin in 1990) and proposed moving to a new location on the northeast corner of Central Park. The corner plot marks the point where Harlem, East Harlem and the Upper East Side converge. It lies to the east of a memorial ellipse dedicated to Duke Ellington and is just outside the Upper Manhattan Empowerment Zone demarcated by federal, state and municipal agencies in 1994.

The new MAA extends Museum Mile, a stretch of cultural properties that begins with the Metropolitan Museum of Art and presently ends with the Museo del Barrio.

Bernard Tschumi's proposal houses 60,000 square-feet of exhibition space within a sheer glass enclosure. Seen through the curtainwall is a wave of wood veneer, fashioned in a stylized replica of the great mud mosques of Mali—with the rod rigging holding up the glass cube approximating the palmwood staves of the original. The sheer walls open the museum to extensive views of Calvert Vaux's Harlem Meer.

The design is still evolving, and the current program calls for permanent and temporary galleries, educational facilities, an auditorium, a museum shop, a café, and an event-space and roof garden.

03.

01.

02.

The Studio Museum in Harlem

144 West 125th Street
Rogers Marvel Architects
2004 Completion

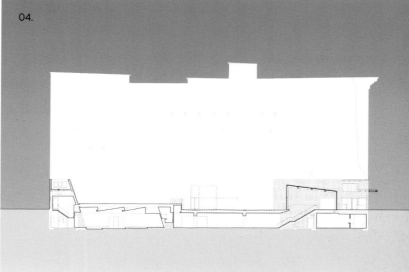

The Studio Museum in Harlem (SMH) is the principal cultural institution in New York City devoted to the work of visual artists of African ancestry, primarily from within the United States, but also encompassing the entire diaspora in the western hemisphere. Lodged in the spiritual heart of African-American culture in North America, the present museum is on the south side of 125th Street, between Lenox Avenue and Adam Clayton Powell Boulevard. The museum's growing permanent collection includes some 1,600 works of art—featuring the work of Jacob Lawrence, James VanDerZee, Romare Bearden, Hale Woodruff, and Richard Hunt—and hosts up to a dozen temporary exhibitions annually.

The Studio Museum first occupied a rented loft off of Fifth Avenue in 1968 and then moved to its present location, donated by the New York Bank for Savings in 1979. The ongoing improvements at the site expand the physical plant from 60,000 square-feet to 72,000 square-feet and are scheduled for completion in 2004. The Manhattan firm of Robert Rogers and Jonathan Marvel, veterans of a number of large-scale cultural projects at the offices of Richard Meier and I. M. Pei & Partners, and the authors of an unrealized master plan for the Louis Armstrong House and Archives in Corona, Queens, was selected for the project.

Enclosed within a new facade of steel and translucent glass at the foot of an existing six-story brick shell, the first phase of the implementation included a sculpture garden, a revamped entry sequence, and the renovation of 3,200-square-feet of exhibtion program for seasonal shows on the first and second floors. Building below grade, the current phase adds 3,000 square-feet of gallery space for the permanent collection, a 100-seat auditorium, a 700 square-foot cafe, and nearly 7,000-square-feet of reading rooms, archives, offices and support spaces.

01. View to west on 125th Street.

02. View of the museum gift shop from the street.

03. The museum occupies the lower floors of a six-story commerical building.

04. Section looking west.

Columbia University Lerner Hall

2920 Broadway
Bernard Tschumi Architects
1999

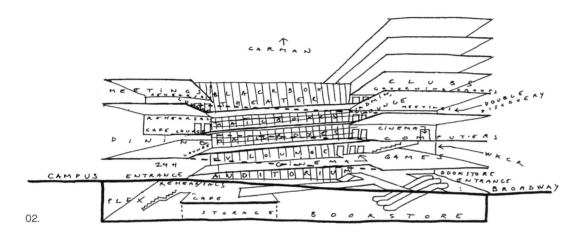

02.

Realized during Bernard Tschumi's tenure as the dean of Columbia's School of Architecture, Planning and Preservation, the Alfred Lerner Hall Student Center is one of a number of academic buildings inserted into the core of McKim, Mead and White's 1897 master plan in the last twenty years. Completed in 1999, it also marks Tschumi's first construction in the United States.

The center organizes a number of student services and activities previously scattered throughout the campus. Two contextual elevations face Broadway and Butler Library, employing a mix of red brick, pale-colored granite and glass blocks. In plan, the scheme takes an exterior public courtyard that the 1897 plan had envisaged between two buildings, and translates it into a series of enclosed public spaces built around a central atrium. Using a dual system of opposed ramps, this hub links the split-level wings into a continuous circuit, thereby joining disparate floors and activities into a

unified space. To tie the building's functions with the rest of the campus, the hub is enclosed to the north by a glass wall—composed of 800-pound, point-supported panes—stretched between the two masonry wings. Sunlight filters through the suspended glass ramps during the day, while at night backlit figures moving along the ramps are visible from outside, making the social space one of both exchange and exhibition.

The program includes an 1,100-seat auditorium and a 400-seat cinema, which can be combined into a 1,500-seat assembly hall by stowing a movable wall. The building also houses lounges, meeting rooms, and a bookstore, as well as dining and kitchen facilities, a radio station, student club areas, game rooms, a nightclub, administrative spaces, a black box theater, six thousand mailboxes, and expanded computer facilities for student use.

01. View of hub and ramp systems.
02. Sketch through hub looking south.
03. View to south on Broadway.

03.

271

06.

04. The 1,100-seat auditorium and 400-seat cinema
can be combined into a 1,500-seat assembly
hall by retracting a movable wall.

05. North elevation.

06. View of north elevation at night, during
a performance staged atop the ramps.

07.

07. The translucent glass paving of the ramps are
illuminated from underneath. View looking east.

08. View looking out to quadrangle.

01.

02.

GEORGE EDMOND ALIN[?]
[?]N JORDAN BAM[?]
FREDE[?]
WILLIAM JOSEPH CLARK J[?]
JERRY J. CHER[?]
GLENN STANLEY DUNBAR
WILLIAM CLANCY EV[?]
[?]NN CHARLES FEINBERG
LEO MIT[?]
GEORGE HENRY FRITZ
JAMES PARSONS GAFFORD JR.
[?]R. SIGMU[?]
[?]ENCE ELMORE GITTINS
[?]BER
KENNETH GORDON LEE

03.

04.

Columbia University War Memorial

116th Street
Architectural Research Office
Design Completed 2000

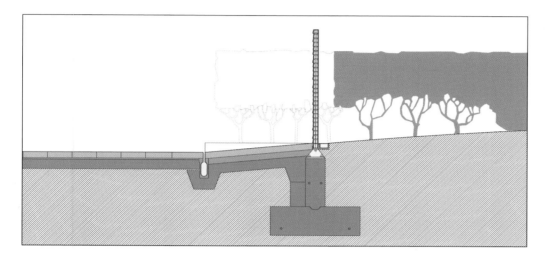

05.

The winning entry in a design competition held in 2000, this memorial honors all Columbia University undergraduates who died in combat in the service of the United States Armed Forces. Using elements familiar to the campus, such as hedge, brick and limestone, it creates discrete spaces for contemplation in keeping with the McKim, Mead and White master plan.

The memorial site—adjacent to a busy campus walkway—is a rectangular grass plot with a sycamore tree at its center. A surrounding 42-inch hedge is cut away at five points to reveal five bronze walls, representing wars waged before 1900, World War I, World War II, the Korean War and the Vietnam War.

Similar to a tree's rings, the walls radiate from the center as the conflicts they commemorate advance through two centuries. The walls also vary in size as they are composed of individual bronze bricks, each bearing the name of a single student who was lost.

The brick faces curve slightly outward, altering the appearance of the walls in different light conditions. The strong shadows cast by direct sunlight highlight the individual bricks, while diffuse light makes the walls seem more monolithic.

The canopy of the sycamore tree further defines the memorial space. Limestone benches connect to the walls, providing spaces for quiet reflection.

01. View looking south, across the quadrangle to Butler Library.

02. Detail of bronze bricks with individual names inscribed on each surface.

03. View looking north.

04. The longest wall, commemorating World War II.

05. Wall section.

01.

02.

Melrose Community Center

286 East 156th Street
Agrest and Gandelsonas Architects
2001

Built for the New York City Housing Authority on a site adjacent to three city housing projects, the Melrose Community Center in the South Bronx provides neighborhood children and teens with 20,000 square-feet of after-school facilities.

Located on the grounds of the Melrose Houses, the complex consists of a large elliptical structure—containing a gymnasium, locker rooms and game rooms—and a bar-shaped wing that houses a library, audiovisual facilities, rooms for computing and arts and crafts, a cafeteria, and administrative offices. The two buildings are linked by a thin "neck" that acts as a common entrance as well as an exhibition space. The plan's diagonal orientation echoes that of the nearby Morrisania Houses on Morris Avenue, while the entry space runs parallel to 156th Street, opening the building to the Andrew Jackson Houses across the street.

The prominent oval form of the gymnasium creates a strong visual presence in the neighborhood while its location on the corner affirms that the center belongs to the housing development. Placing the gymnasium in a

separate structure also allows use of the facilities to be compartmentalized—when an athletic event is taking place, the other areas can be closed, or vice versa.

The bar-shaped building is designed for maximum transparency. Curtainwall glazing exposes the interior to public view, while glass interior walls divide the different rooms from a circulation spine located on the building's periphery. An exterior video screen linked to the building's audiovisual facility also provides a venue for public showings of videos produced at the center.

01. Northeast view with Andrew Jackson Houses.

02. Classroom wing, view looking east to Melrose Housing Complex.

03. Exploded axonometric diagram.

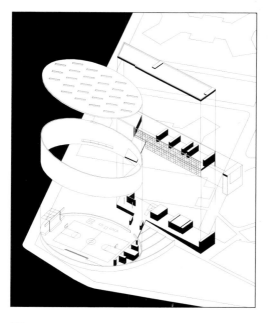

03.

04.

05.

06.

04. - 05. Views of the rear of the center.

06. The "neck" linking the two halves of the complex.

07. Second-floor library.

08. Activity room.

09. Entry sequence, view to south.

07.

08.

09.

01.

02.

Lehman College Physical Education Facility

Bedford Park West Boulevard, Bronx
Rafael Viñoly Architects
1994

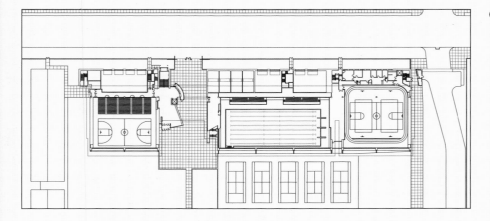

03.

This new gymnasium for the City University of New York's Herbert H. Lehman College lies just east of the Jerome Park reservoir, on the corner of Bedford Park and Goulden boulevards in north Bronx. It is one of a number of public buildings in the borough designed by Rafael Viñoly in the last ten years, including the Bronx Housing Courthouse on 1118 Grand Concourse (1997) and the Bronx Criminal Courthouse on 161st Street (2003).

Aligned with Bedford Park Boulevard, the longitudinal axis of the 142,000-square-foot building defines the uppermost edge of the Neo-Gothic campus, occupying a rectangular plot the width of Harris Park to the north. The entire athletic program, consisting of two gymnasiums, an Olympic-size swimming pool, a ballet theater and auxiliary facilities, is housed under an immense, stainless-steel hangar, propped up by exposed trusses painted white.

The building's singular form has become an icon of the college to the neighborhood, its play of light and heavy forms articulating a sequence of dramatic profiles. In a sweeping gesture, the segmented arc of the great roof—set at near grade on the campus side—rises to form a crest over the street side. Forty-feet high, the north-facing elevation is supported by a concrete and glass volume containing classrooms and administrative offices. A cutout on the south facade encloses a lobby and a grand stair, which together form the main entry. Natural light is introduced through a continuous clerestory, its transparency contrasting with the opaque surfaces of the building exterior throughout the day.

01. Main entry along south elevation.

02. View looking east.

03. Ground floor plan.

04. Campus view with Harris Park on the upper left.

04.

MoMA QNS

33rd Street and Queens Boulevard, Long Island City
Michael Maltzan Architects
Cooper Roberston and Partners
Base
2002

In 1999, the Museum of Modern Art acquired the former Swingline Staple Factory on 33rd Street and Queens Boulevard in anticipation of the four-year renovation of its midtown headquarters. Opened in June 2002, MoMA QNS is the interim base for all the museum's operations and exhibition programs through 2005, and a permanent storage facility for its vast art holdings.

Designed by Michael Maltzan Architecture and Scott Newman of Cooper Robertson and Partners, MoMA QNS incorporates 160,000 square-feet of program inside the former industrial space, of which 25,000 square-feet are dedicated to exhibitions. Apart from gallery and collection management functions, the converted structure also supports a new conservation lab, administrative offices, imaging and framing facilities, a library, a museum store, and a cafe.

The subway commute from Manhattan to Long Island City, a transitional environment that Michael Maltzan describes as the "middle lanscape" between metropolis and suburb, is an important experiential component that informs the design. As visitors traveling on the elevated No. 7 Local subway approach, rooftop panels with the letters of the MoMA logo come in to view, and as the train pulls into the 33rd street station, the letters come together in an homage to the traditional super-graphics of the area's bygone industrial age. Alighting from the subway platform, visitors are led by patterned lighting elements half a block to the museum entrance. Confronted with an expanse of blue stucco (referencing the bright azure brick of the old Swingline factory), museumgoers access the lobby through an operable wall of sliding glass doors. They then proceed to the information desk and into the galleries, or else ascend up a ramp to the museum store and cafe.

The layout of the gallery spaces is flexible: Only the perimeter wall is fixed, and walls can be reconstructed within the 21-foot-high spaces to accommodate variable exhibition requirements. The nonpublic spaces have been tailored for the 125 employees who work on-site. The museum's library and archives are housed in a well-lit space for its nearly 200,000 volumes, and for a double-height public reading room with views out to 33rd Street.

01. The elevated 33rd Street Station of the No. 7 Subway overlooks the principal facade.

02. View towards
    entrance ramp.

03. Ticketing and
    information desk.

04. Ticketing desk
    viewed from mez-
    zanine level.

03.

05. The walls of the
    lobby extend
    beyond the bound-
    ary set by the
    sloping floor and
    appear to hover
    over the ticketing
    desk. Projections
    expand the exhibi-
    tion space by
    including the entry
    sequence.

06. Mezzanine-level
    gift shop viewed
    from the foot of
    the ramp.

04.

07.

08.

09.

07. Entrance elevation.

08. Perspective view
    at dusk.

09. Roofscape viewed
    from the elevated
    subway platform.
    The graphic identi-
    ty was developed
    by Base in collabo-
    ration with the
    architects.

10. A dedicated lab
    provides conserva-
    tors with the best
    conditions in which
    to clean and repair
    works of art.

10.

01.

02.

03.

P. S. 1 Expansion

22-25 Jackson Avenue & 46th Street
Frederick Fisher
1997

P. S. 1 Dunescape

Sharples Holden Pasquarelli
2000

Founded in 1971, P. S. 1 Contemporary Art Center is one of the largest institutions in the United States devoted solely to the advancement of contemporary art. It has mounted some of the most provocative visual-arts exhibitions of the last quarter century, and distinguishes itself from other major art museums in its progressive approach to exhibitions and its involvement of artists within its organizational framework. Housed in a converted Neo-Romanesque schoolhouse in Long Island City, two subway stops from the new MoMA QNS, the complex underwent an extensive three-year renovation in the 1990s. Under the direction of Los Angeles-based architect Frederick Fisher, P. S. 1 expanded its physical plant to 125,000 square-feet, reopening in 1997 with a new entry sequence, a large outdoor gallery, and a two-story project space.

In 1999, The Museum of Modern Art formalized an operational affiliation with P. S. 1, and in the following year, initiated the Young Architects Program, an annual competition that invites emerging designers to realize projects in a triangular courtyard framed by Fisher's concrete interventions. The New York firm

Sharples Holden Pasquarelli (ShoP) was awarded the inaugural prize for Warm Up 2000, and the installation lasted all summer.

The dunescape design provides an alternative way to enjoy the urban summer. Creating an experience inspired by vacations by the sea, museumgoers are invited to mingle, bathe, work on their tan, or walk through a spray of water mist to cool off. Several programmatic elements—cabana, beach chair, umbrella, boogie board, and surf—are positioned along a composite wood structure, a hybrid of boardwalk and beach comprised of over 6,000 individual 2-foot-by-2-foot cedar strips. SHoP describes a vinyl surface "that bends and folds to accommodate various spatial configurations. When the surface is high in the air, it provides shade; when it is lower, it provides inclined seating areas. When it is on its side, it becomes a thickened translucent wall, creating individual 'cabanas' where visitors may change their clothing." As it twists onto the ground, "lifeguard" stands also serve as "dancing" platforms. Water runs along the entire surface, collecting in pools throughout the courtyard where wood makes contact with the pavement.

01. Interior view of expanded gallery.

02. View above dunescape, summer 2000.

03. View looking west to Manhattan.

04. Dunescape, view looking west.

05. Detail: shower rooms.

06. Roof detail.

07. The installation lasted through
the summer of 2000.

05.

06.

07.

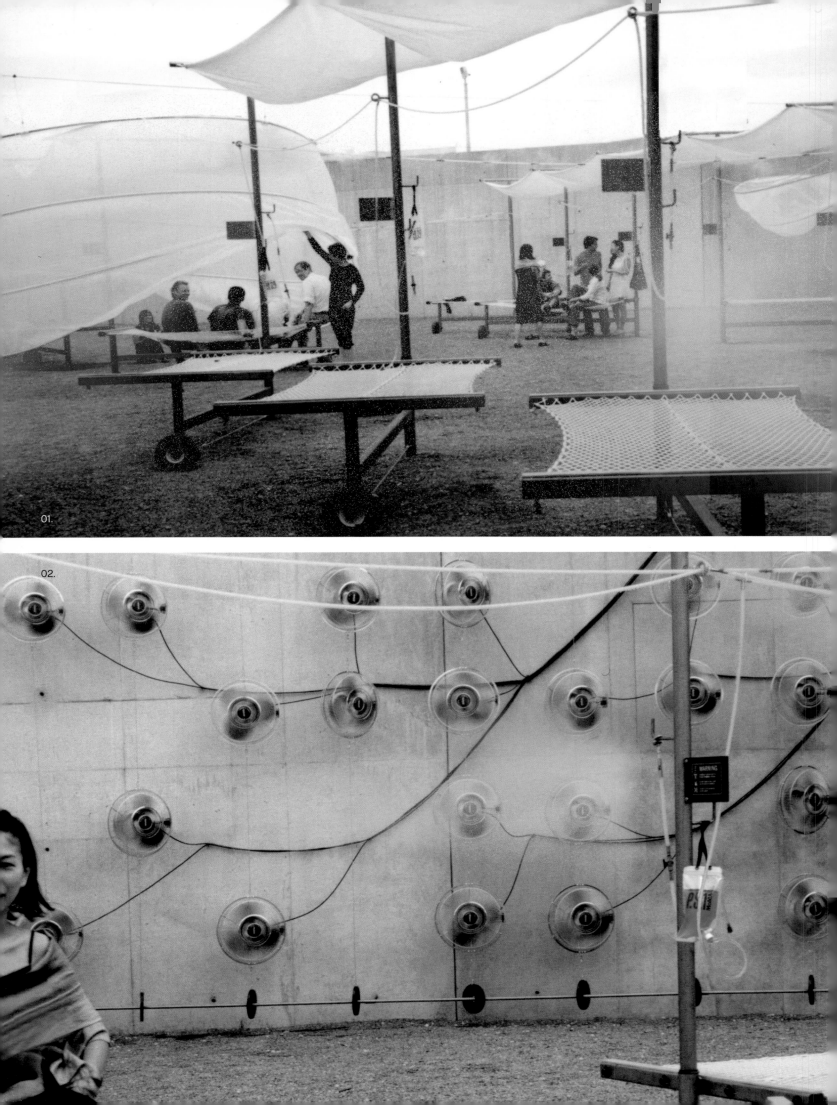

01.

02.

P. S. 1 SubWave

22-25 Jackson Avenue & 46th Street, Queens
ROY
2001

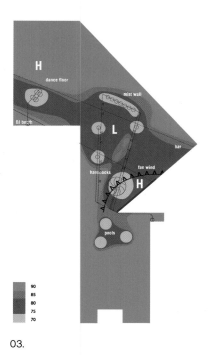

03.

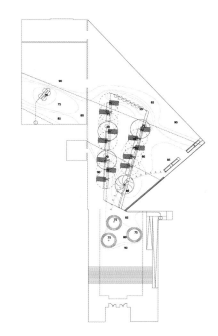

04.

Lindy Roy's winning entry in the second annual P. S. 1/MoMA Young Architects Program competition was conceived as a flexible stage for an annual series of summer events. In particular, the scheme readily adapts to two operational conditions: For eight Saturdays in July and August P. S. 1 is transformed into an open-air club where DJs spin for up to five thousand guests; during the week, it serves as an oasis for urbanites to relax and escape the heat.

A series of climate modifiers are introduced into the concrete courtyard: wind, spray, water and shade are distributed, forming microclimates. Forty-five stainless-steel fans—strung on tension cables and weighted—oscillate to mimic variable wind conditions. Spray machines simulate fog, further cooling the air.

Twelve daybeds—propped on a steel frame, anchored to a 10-foot tube, strung with knotless nylon mesh, and mounted on pneumatic tires—can be pivoted 360 degrees in and out of the shade of a UV-rated canopy. Blue neoprene strips line the steel frame to form a cushioned headrest. Each daybed is furnished with hydration packs, towels and a personal atomizer linked to the spray infrastructure. Complete with shoulder straps and hands-free drinking straws, hydration packs can be worn while moving about or hung like IV bags off hooks welded onto the frame. Cylindrical scrims made of iridescent fiber are suspended from tension cables—PVC hoops sixteen feet in diameter shape their soft armature. Scrims can be dropped over pairs of hammocks, creating more intimate spaces. A showerhead rains water in front of the fans and onto a pavement of loose, white pebbles.

01. Daybeds in the mist.

02. Fans mounted along courtyard wall.

03. Temperature plan.

04. Site plan.

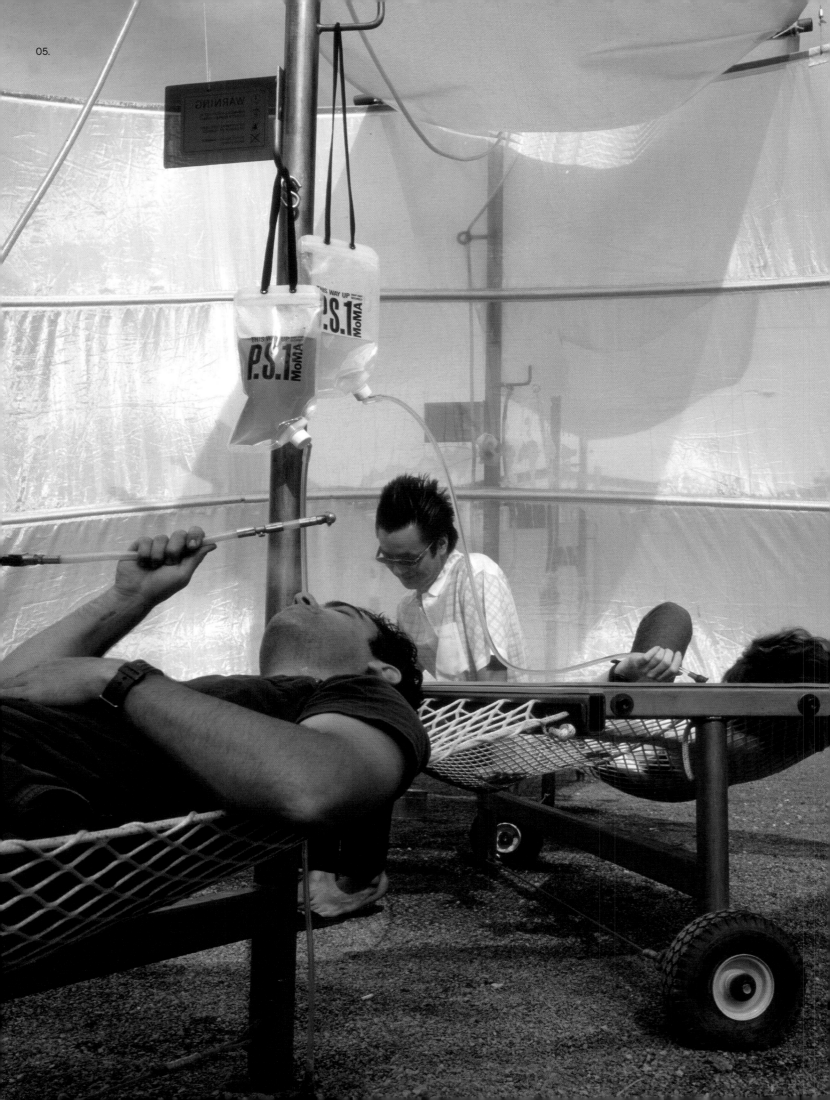

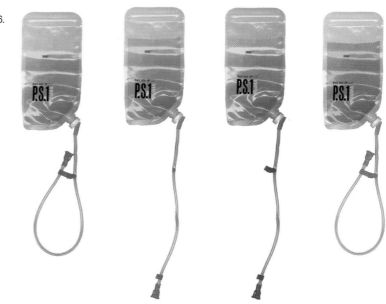

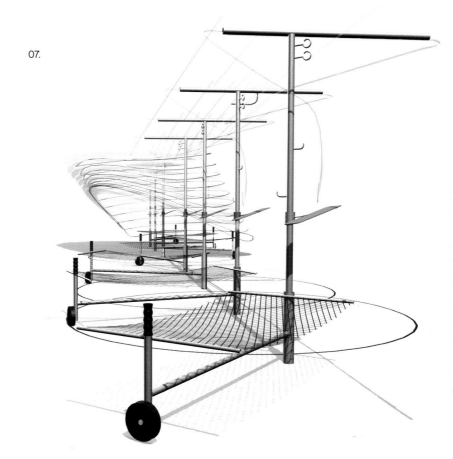

05. Daybeds, scrim enclosures, mist machines and electric fans create a custom microclimate.

06. Hydration packs in the form of IV bags hang from hooks welded onto the daybed frame.

07. Mounted on pneumatic tires, the daybeds can rotate 360 degrees to meet the shade.

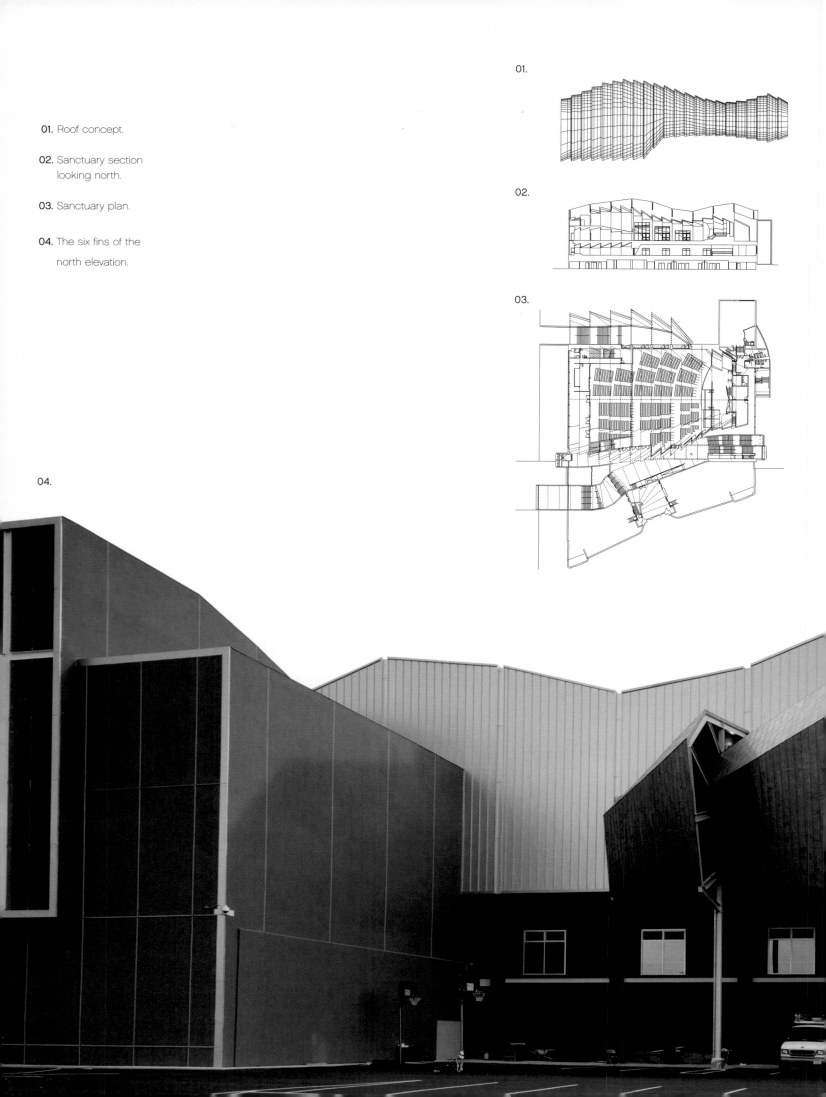

01. Roof concept.

02. Sanctuary section looking north.

03. Sanctuary plan.

04. The six fins of the north elevation.

01.

02.

03.

04.

Korean Presbyterian Church

43-05 37th Avenue, Queens
Greg Lynn FORM
Douglas Garofalo Architects
Michael McInturf Architects
1999

The first field test of Greg Lynn's digital experiments in animate form, the Korean Presbyterian Church of New York in Sunnyside, Queens, was actually conducted by three separate practices working out of three different cities: Douglas Garofalo Architects in Chicago, Michael McInturf Architects in Cincinnati and Greg Lynn FORM (at the time, in Hoboken, New Jersey, and now in Los Angeles). Interconnectivity bridged the physical distances and enabled the team to execute a project too large and complex for any one of its constituent firms to accomplish on its own.

Adjacent to the tracks of the Long Island Railroad, the new church is part renovation and new construction, organized around the Streamline Moderne shell of the Knickerbocker Laundry Factory built in 1936. The reuse of a neglected industrial building as a place of worship and a community center for the Korean-American congregants involved a comprehensive survey of the existing conditions. Lynn and company then proposed linking the original building to an immense, new assembly area with intermediate structures.

05. Grand staircase
leading up to the
main sanctuary.

06. Hallway ouside
sanctuary.

07. Sanctuary interior.

The new church is contained within the former laundry, and much of its formal idiom is preserved along the south facade. The interior was reconfigured to support a welter of new uses. The sanctuary hosts services for 2,500 people, and the spaces radiating from this central space include a 600-seat wedding chapel, a variety of assembly spaces, a choir rehearsal space, a cafeteria, a library, a day-care center, and eighty classrooms—used primarily by the parishioners, but are open to area schools and other neighborhood groups for secular functions.

The interventions are protected by a new roof structure, fashioned out of metal panels, and attached to the host structure like a giant steel remora. Expressed dramatically along the northern elevation—where it shelters a grand stair leading down from the sanctuary to the main parking lot—the roof nearly makes contact with the ground, perforated and flared like the gills of a shark.

09.

10.

11.

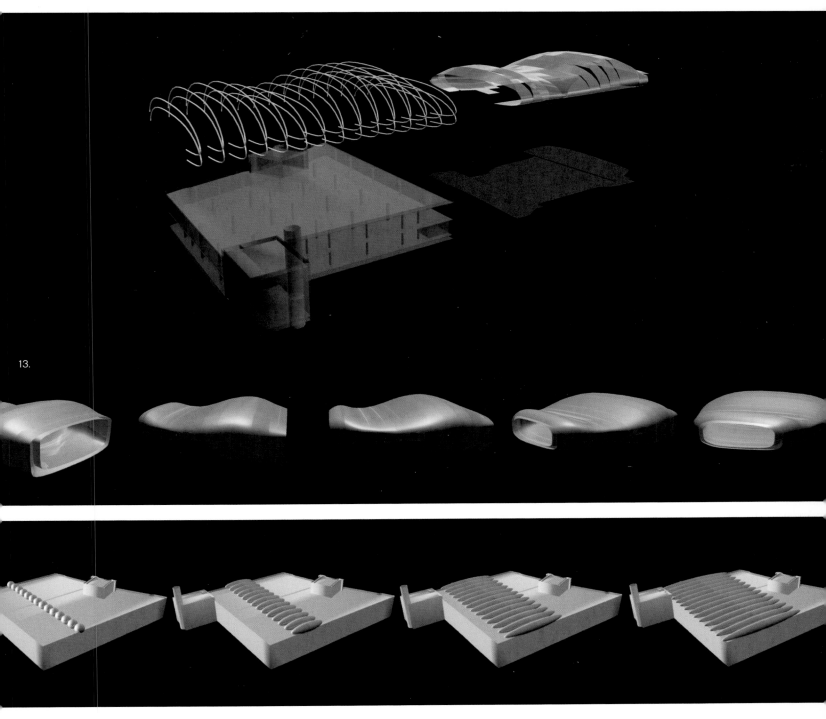

12.

13.

14.

08. Conceptual model of the "blob" housing the new sanctuary and building circulation.

09. - 11. Views of the open carapace over the outdoor stair.

12. - 14. The "blob" is positioned over the existing Knickerbocker Laundry Building.

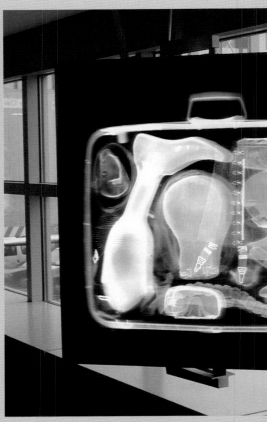

Travelogues

JFK International Airport Terminal 4
Diller + Scofidio
2001

This series of interventions was the winning entry in a competition to create site-specific artwork within Terminal 4 of the International Arrivals Building at JFK International Airport. With a little whimsy, Diller + Scofidio crafted specific responses to the nature of the sterile corridor, a featureless transitional space that conveys air travelers toward the customs and passport control stations after deplaning.

The permanent installation consists of thirty-three lenticular screens—seven in the east wing and twenty-six in the west wing—placed at even intervals along the 1,800 feet of corridor. Each screen holds one second of action that is animated by the speed of the moving viewer. The succession of screens builds a sequence of micro movies, with the spaces between them forming time lapses. As they move along the corridor, travelers inadvertently engage in a real-time visual narrative. Each lenticular screen is a ribbed sheet consisting of hundreds of cylindrical lenses, with parallel images compressed beneath them, capable of producing a picture with motion and depth. As the eye travels past, the lenses refract the images, revealing a sequence and generating an animated, three-dimensional effect. Lenticular technology requires significantly less maintenance than a similar electronic or video installation.

The panels tell fictional narratives through passengers' luggage. Suitcases, chosen at random from airport travelers, are X-rayed, and as their contents materialize they trigger flashback images of travel experiences, before the screens move on to focus on the next traveler's baggage.

01. - 04. Installations along west wing of JFK Terminal 4.

05. Sequence from "The Suitcase."

01.

02.

P. S. 42 / The L!brary Initiative

488 Beach 66th Street, Queens
Weiss / Manfredi Architects
2002

03.

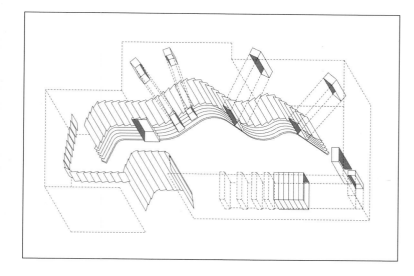

The L!brary Initiative is part of a much larger effort to reverse patterns of low literacy and scholastic underachievement among children in New York City. Alarmed by figures indicating that up to 60 percent of public school students in grades 3 through 8 were reading below grade level, the Robin Hood Foundation—a nonprofit organization launched to "target the sources of poverty" in the city—formed a partnership with the mayor's office, the Board of Education, a dozen architectural practices, a graphic design firm, two major children's book publishers, and other corporate sponsors to design, outfit and staff new libraries in existing elementary schools. The project is dedicated to the transformation of the school library into a critical resource for the entire community—a site where pupils, teachers and parents work together in improving student performance.

The Robin Hood Foundation approached Henry Myerberg, principal at Helfand Myerberg Guggenheimer, who in turn enlisted a team of nine other architectural firms in providing design services pro bono in the creation of the first ten spaces. With a budget of about $1 million per school, each volunteer firm was assigned one prototype library. Ten pilot libraries opened through the spring of 2003, with another twenty planned through schoolyear 2004-05.

The New York firm of Marion Weiss and Michael Manfredi was part of the inaugural group of L!brary Initiative architects, and their library for P. S. 42 in Queens was completed in the fall of 2002. Located in Far Rockaway, Queens, P. S. 42 was a particularly troubled school, with 4th grade reading test scores well below the citywide average, and a cramped, inaccessible library stacked with several thousand out-of-date books. Nearly doubling its size, the new scheme relocates the library from the fourth floor to ground level, next to the main school entrance and cafeteria. Converted from an underused gym, the new library is now centrally positioned, visible from the street, and is open daily until 5 PM.

Conceived by the architects as an "occupiable bookworm," the library is defined by a curving wall of finished plywood running the length of the room. Restocked with new books, the wall is punctuated by deep windows, with wide ledges that can serve as impromptu benches. Inherently flexible, the space can be reconfigured to support multiple functions. A translucent scrim—printed with the letters of the alphabet—can be drawn and shut like a shower curtain to create an enclosed storytelling area, or an open backdrop for performances and presentations. Shelves and plush seats mounted on casters can be moved around to open up the space for larger events.

01. View along the curvilinear plywood wall.

02. Detail of movable shelves.

03. Axonometric diagram: Shelving plan.

04.

05.

06.

04. The pattern printed on the hanging scrim.

05. Mobile furnishings allow for a high degree of programmatic flexibility. Shelves can be compacted to accommodate community events.

06. Deep windows are visible behind the deployed scrim.

07. The scrim can be drawn to create a storytelling enclosure.

01.

02.

Pratt Institute
Higgins Hall Center Wing

Lafayette Avenue at St. James Place, Brooklyn
Steven Holl Architects
2004 Completion

03.

01. Perspective view.

02. Interior view looking out to street.

03. East elevation.

04. Aerial view of Higgins Hall.

In 1996, a four-alarm fire damaged the center section of Higgins Hall, a building that houses key functions of the Pratt Institute's architectural school. This project uses the reconstruction as an opportunity to rethink the building's programmatic elements and transform fundamental relationships between its main spatial and programmatic components.

In the original building configuration—an "H" plan with three segments and center courts facing east and west—the floor plates of the north wing and south wing do not align. Their variance increases with each floor, from a mere half-inch at ground level to a seven-foot disparity between the fourth floors.

For the renovation, concrete floor planks sheathed in walls of white glass grow out of the north and south wings at points

corresponding to each building's floor plates. As these planks extend inward toward one another, the design opens up to mediate between the dissonant floor plates with panes of clear glass, allowing views toward the east court and creating a coherent central entrance at the west court. A two-part skylight tops this section, joining north light with south light at the juncture of the building's extant wings.

The 22,500-square-foot structure contains a lobby, a gallery, an auditorium, studios, a workshop, a digital resource center, and a review room. The base uses recycled brick from the burned section of the building to form a new entrance court and a viewing terrace. The industrial white glass transmits diffuse natural light into the building by day and lends it a translucent glow at night.

04.

Brooklyn Museum of Art Expansion

200 Eastern Parkway, Brooklyn
Polshek Partnership
2004 Completion

02.

Housing over 1.5 million works of art, the Brooklyn Museum of Art (BMA) is one of the largest institutions of its type, renowned for its encyclopedic collections of Americana and ancient Egyptian art. The BMA faces Eastern Parkway and occupies the northeast corner of a 52-acre urban wedge it shares with the Brooklyn Botanic Garden, which was formed out of Olmsted and Vaux's 526-acre Prospect Park. The Museum is currently engaged in a major building program, which in the last two decades saw the expansion of its physical plant from the 450,000 square-feet of the original McKim, Mead and White core—built in 1897—to accommodate an additional 127,000 square-feet. Much of this activity is interested in increasing visitor traffic, and improving the civic spaces of the museum, important components of a 25-year master plan initiated in 1986.

The Polshek Partnership has been involved throughout the history of the ongoing development as part of the original master plan design team—with Arata Isozaki & Associates—and as principal architects for renovations at the landmark structure. Within the last decade, the firm enlarged the Egyptian wing, added a new 460-seat auditorium, and restored the central Beaux-Arts court.

The latest phase is a thorough redesign of the pedestrian sequence along Eastern Parkway. James Polshek's scheme organizes all the BMA's recent additions around a new entrance pavilion directly underneath the central portico. Commanding a new landscaped plaza with watercourses, the 7,000-square-foot structure doubles the existing lobby space of the museum. It is conceived as a low dome with a curved glass-and-steel roof and walls of point-supported laminated glass on a nonlinear, tension-supported structure. The pavilion replaces the footprint of the grand staircase—demolished in 1934—that once took museum visitors from the avenue all the way up to the third floor. Twice the height of the stair in front of the Metropolitan Museum, the trustees of the BMA endorsed the idea of an entirely new construction, and argued that replicating the original staircase was contrary to the idea of increased accessibility, particularly in view of the requirements mandated by the Americans with Disabilities Act.

01. View looking up the glass roof of the new entrance pavilion.

02. 39 cherry trees—replacing the copse uprooted in 2002—and new fountains are envisaged for the new plaza.

03. The new entry is the second phase of a project that began in the late 1990s. The features of the first phase included additional parking and a proposed outdoor gallery for the BMA's collection of architectural fragments from lost New York City buildings. As construction on the Eastern Parkway facade is planned through 2004, a new south entry was recently opened to provide access to the collections.

03.

01.

02.

BAM Rose Cinema and Cafe

30 Lafayette Avenue
Hardy Holzman Pfeiffer Associates
1998

Founded in 1861, the Brooklyn Academy of Music (BAM) is America's oldest performing arts center. After fire destroyed its previous facility, the Academy moved into its present building in 1908, designed by architects Herts and Tallant. As part of a comprehensive overhaul of its public spaces, the recent interior reconfiguration fosters a more efficient use of public space as it capably restores the grandeur of the theatergoing experience.

Adapting the building's original circulation patterns, the design returns the second floor to public use through the creation of the BAM Cafe. The principal gathering space for the BAM's upper level, this soaring room—punctuated by vaulted trusswork arches that echo the building's five exterior windows—operates as a bar and restaurant while offering the flexibility to host live music performances and parties. A new glass-enclosed shop to one side of the Cafe allows BAM patrons to purchase books, compact disks, and souvenirs.

HHPA's improvements also include the transformation of an underutilized but architecturally significant playhouse into four movie theaters that showcase independent and foreign films. Known collectively as BAM Rose Cinemas, the complex features an interior lobby area with restored woodwork and arched entry vaults. Two ground-floor theaters seat 103 and 155 people, and two larger mezzanine-level cinemas contain 230 and 272 seats. With clean sight-lines and coffered ceilings—as well as an ornate proscenium arch in one of the upper-level cinemas—the theaters arguably provide one of the best movie-watching venues in the city, while state-of-the-art sound and projection equipment allow for a variety of film formats.

It must however be noted that security issues prevent the cinemas from being operationally connected to the cafe. Moviegoers exit downstairs into the main lobby area, from which they can access the cafe through an escalator on the second floor. Silmilarly, cafe patrons must return to the downstairs lobby to gain entrance to the cinemas and the main performance hall.

01. View looking up the illuminated "vaults" HHPA devised for the BAM Cafe.

02. View of one of the movie theaters on the mezzanine level.

03. Exterior view of the principal facade on Lafayette Avenue with views into the cafe on the second floor.

03.

317

Brooklyn Public Library

Flatbush Avenue at Ashland Place
TEN Arquitectos
Design Completed 2002

02.

This $70 million Visual and Performing Arts Library is part of a cluster of buildings and institutions—including the Brooklyn Academy of Music and the Mark Morris Dance Center (Beyer Blinder Belle, 2000)—that together anchor downtown Brooklyn's emerging new cultural district.

Located on a triangular wedge bordered by Flatbush Avenue, Lafayette Street and Ashland Place, the new library responds to the complexities of its site with a prominent V-shaped design. The building's permeable, transparent façades invite public use, while the boldness of the structure helps the library assert its status as an icon of innovation.

The library's façade is a double wall of glass, with horizontal louvers sandwiched between the window panels to control the amount of light transmitted to the interior. The building's skin also changes character throughout course of the day with the fluctuations of natural light conditions. This curtainwall sets up an ongoing visual flow between interior and exterior space, allowing passersby to view the activities inside and forming a collage of space, people and movement. The 150,000-square-foot building within houses reading rooms, archives, galleries, media labs, an auditorium, a theater, and a 24-hour media lounge.

The Flatbush Avenue elevation pulls away like a curtain to reveal an interior plaza, part of a courtyard enclosed by the V-shaped plan, framing views of the Brooklyn Academy of Music beyond. The flight of steps leading to the plaza also serves as an amphitheater.

01. View to northwest along Flatbush Avenue.

02. Section looking east.

03. View to southeast towards Grand Army Plaza.

01.

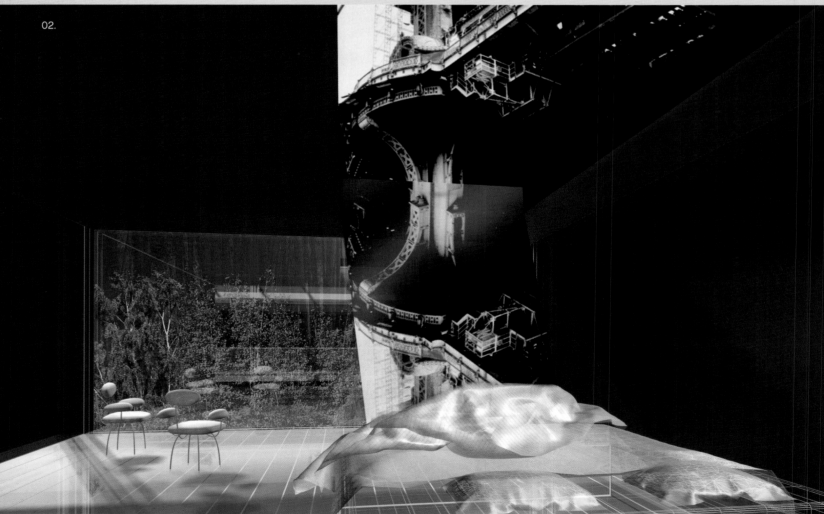

02.

03.

RIVER HOTEL

T.04   T.03   CINEMA COMPLEX   MAIN STREET PIER   T.02   T.01

PHILIPS   BOUCHERON

DUMBO Hotel / Main Street Pier

Fulton Landing waterfront, Brooklyn
Architectures Jean Nouvel
Design Completed 1999

The design for this hotel was commissioned by local real-estate developer David Walentas as part of a plan envisioned for the Brooklyn neighborhood known as DUMBO (Down Under the Manhattan Bridge Overpass). Sited within a currently undeveloped city-owned stretch of waterfront between the Brooklyn and Manhattan bridges, this 377,000-square-foot hotel posits a unique vision for an up-and-coming area while creating a bold gesture across the river toward Manhattan.

Taking cues from its waterfront location, the highly transparent hotel is conceived as a "bridge between bridges" where the 250 rooms cantilever out over the East River and spacious balconies offer ship's angle views of the suspended bridge decks overhead. The hotel projects out over the water like a pier, connecting the neighborhood to its industrial maritime history while appearing to reach out toward the shore of Manhattan. This gesture combines with the hotel's glass curtainwall to hold up a mirrorlike reflection across the river, offering Manhattan a new view of itself.

The west deck of the hotel lobby extends a four-hundred-foot bay window that provides panoramic views of the bridges, the water and the Manhattan skyline. The building houses a health club that overlooks the Brooklyn Bridge, as well as a sixteen-theater cinema in which the screens lift up during intermissions to reveal sweeping river views. The full waterfront complex includes retail shops, parking space and a riverside promenade that winds through a redeveloped waterfront park.

01. Viewing deck under cantelivered volume.

02. Ship's angle view of the Manhattan Bridge from one of the hotel rooms.

03. South elevation.

04. Montage view along East River.

04.

05.

06.

05. Hallway leading to
hotel suites.

06 - 09. Interior views
of hotel suites.

09. View of bi-level hotel
lobby looking south.

324

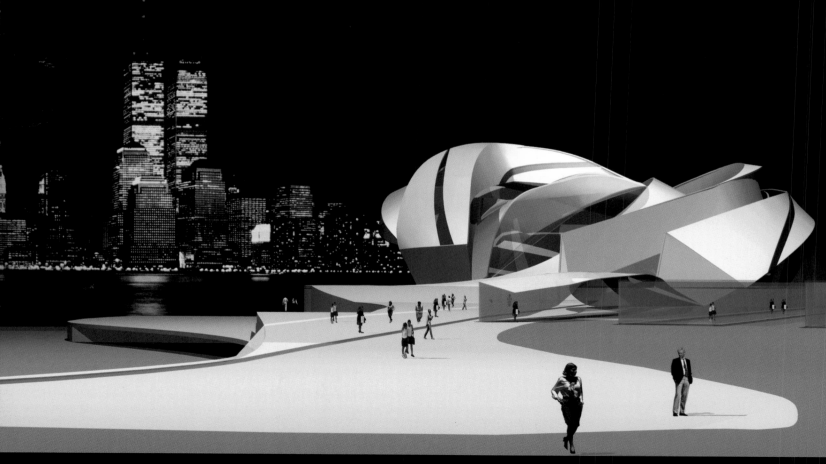

Staten Island Institute for Arts & Sciences

St. George Ferry Terminal, Staten Island
Eisenman Architects
Design Completed 1997

02.

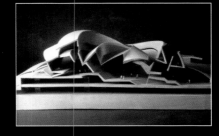

03.

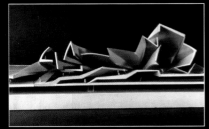

Transforming a vital transport hub into a cultural and artistic center, Peter Eisenman addresses a shift in the nature of the American museum at a time when civic monuments, formerly typified by federal buildings and cultural institutions, have since been supplanted by sports arenas and convention centers.

The St. George Ferry Terminal is the primary gateway to Staten Island—an intermodal transport nexus for bus, train and ferry services. Recent restoration projects—such as those at Grand Central Station in New York and Union Station in Washington, D.C.— have reinvented portions of major transit centers into urban shopping malls and gathering spaces. Here, the restoration and renovation of this terminal presents the opportunity to transform a facility that handles twenty million commuters a year into a driving force for local economic growth and a magnet for cultural development. Located beside the

terminal, the $65 million waterfront museum takes advantage of the terminal's natural pedestrian traffic, but also provides a reason for tourists to disembark from the ferry and spend time on Staten Island. Visitors to the museum will experience interactive state-of-the-art displays as they move beneath a swirling translucent roof structure, and across warped and striated forms that define a series of interlocking layers of space, transforming the spatial experience into a destination without an end. The museum's plaza steps down toward the waterfront, creating a natural outdoor gathering space with postcard views of New York harbor and lower Manhattan.

01. Exterior looking toward Manhattan.

02. - 03. Section models.

04. View from northeast.

04.

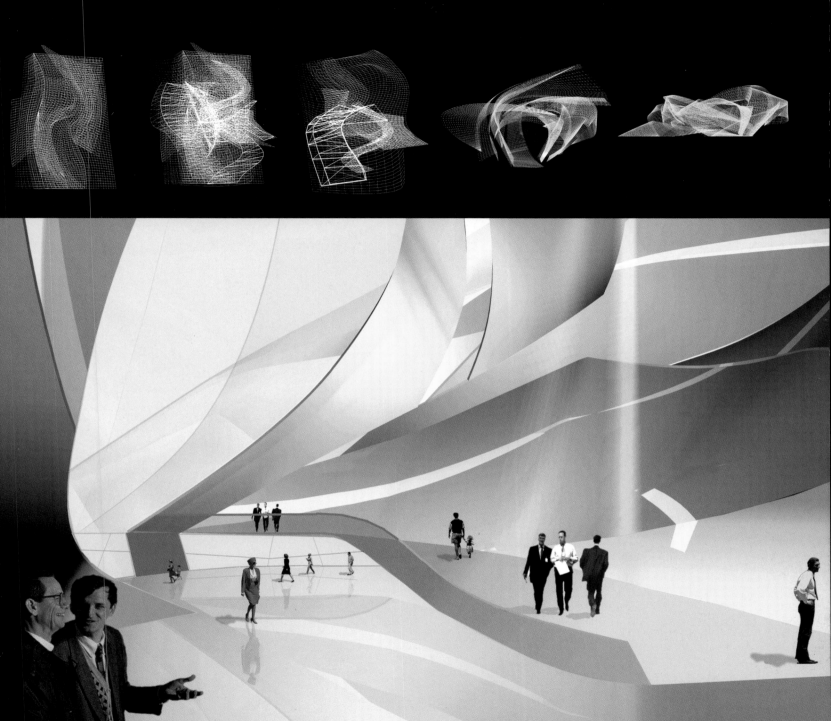

07.

05. Morphological sequence.

06. - 07. Interior views.

01.

02.

Fresh Kills Landfill to Landscape

Fresh Kills Landfill, Staten Island
Field Operations
Design Completed 2001

03.

Until the Giuliani administration decided to sell New York City's garbage out-of-state, the Fresh Kills Landfill was for five decades the largest of its kind in the eastern seaboard. Its mounds visible from the moon, the 2,200-acre facility sat on the western shore of Staten Island, and processed up to 500 tons of refuse an hour.

Not long after the dump officially shut down in March 2001, the Mayor's Office and the Department of City Planning held an open competition to determine the long-term future of the site. Dubbed "Landfill to Landscape," the brief for the master plan sought a phased, flexible "model of land regeneration" that extended the remit of the old dump to cover a swath of land across Arthur Kill, the brackish, saltwater strait separating southwest Staten Island from Woodbridge, New Jersey. An important consideration in reprogramming Fresh Kills was the restoration of the area's original ecosystems—a stretch of tidal wetlands and wooded areas lining the network of creeks winding from the western edge to the center of Staten Island—into a permanent greenspace and a sanctuary for migratory birds.

Field Operations, the firm created by urban planner and landscape architect James Corner and architect Stan Allen, bested a field of six interdisciplinary teams in the final stage of the competition. Their proposal, Lifescape, envisages the transformation of the island from Manhattan's "backyard bypass" to a "nature lifestyle island," with a reclaimed Fresh Kills Reserve as its centerpiece.

In concert with the ecological agenda, the Lifescape plan suggests an extensive recreational program in the form of golf courses, playgrounds, picnic areas, bike trails, an equestrian park, a market, a boardwalk, and a small sports stadium, arranged along the West Shore Expressway. As the process of restoring the natural habitat—and eliminating contaminated runoff—will take three decades, some of these leisure amenities are expected to open early in the implementation of the enormous project.

In the wake of the terrorist attack on September 11, 2001, the former landfill became the staging area for a crucial stage in the recovery effort. Debris and material evidence from the World Trade Center were brought by barge and truck to Fresh Kills—and three other salvage yards in New Jersey—to be sorted. At the close of the six-month investigation, the steel and concrete remains of the towers were ultimately incorporated into the biggest mound in the landfill.

Field Operations revised their scheme to include a memorial surmounting the elevated site, in the form of huge, inclined berms. Set on a field of wildflowers and on an axis pointing to Ground Zero, the length of these earthworks match the height of the fallen towers. Approached by trails linked to the new park areas, the mounds are inset with small markers inscribed with the names of the dead.

01. View along Richmond Creek looking west. A proposed heron nesting site is in foreground.

02. View looking north with Arthur Kill and New Jersey to the left.

03. The memorial to the World Trade Center recovery effort conducted at the landfill.

331

01.

02.

03.

04.

05.

A New World Trade Center

Tribute in Light

Independently authored by a number of design teams in the wake of the World Trade Center attacks, the two massive beams of light—cast by 88 spotlights—that comprised this temporary memorial were projected from a site north of where the two towers once stood, and illumined the night sky above lower Manhattan from March 11 to April 13, 2002.

Produced with the assistance of the Battery Park Authority, the Municipal Arts Society and Creative Time, "Tribute in Light" was a collaboration between John Bennett and Gustavo Bonevardi of PROUN Space Studio, lighting designers Fisher Marantz Stone, architect Richard Nash-Gould, and artists Julian LaVerdiere and Paul Myoda—who both participated in the Lower Manhattan Cultural Council's World Views artist residency program formerly located on the 91st floor of World Trade Center Tower One.

Page 332

01. View of the recovery effort at the WTC site.

02. - 04. Views taken during the official unveiling of the temporary memorial, March 11, 2002.

05. Perspective from New York Harbor.

Max Protetch Gallery

Max Protetch organized a provocative exhibition of World Trade Center designs at his Chelsea gallery from January 17 to February 16, 2002; and at the National Building Museum in Washington, D. C. from April 6 to June 10, 2002.

For the New York show, Protetch and co-curator Aaron Betsky—assisted by staff at both *Architecture* and *Architectural Record* magazines—sought contributions from a global cross-section of architectural practices and artists in the fall of 2001. Of the 125 firms and individuals they approached, nearly sixty provided drawings, models and interactive multimedia presentations.

Entitled "A New World Center: Design Proposals from Leading Architects Worldwide," the show catalogued a specific community's response to the tragic events of the previous year. Outside the remit of any officially recognized agency engaged in the rebuilding of lower Manhattan, the exhibition presented the site as an unprecedented opportunity for renewal and innovation. At a time when the viability of the skyscraper as a type was in doubt, many of the explorations were in the form of memorials and mixed-use towers that achieved or exceeded the proportions of Minoru Yamasaki's original towers.

Page 335

06. - 07. Steven Holl Architects: Folded Street and Floating Memorial.

08. One of the 81 scenarios generated by Arch-Tectonic's Flex-City, NYC 1991-2012.

New York Times Magazine and *New York*

Around the first anniversary of September 11th, the *New York Times Magazine* and *New York* magazine published designs for the World Trade Center site. Submitted at the invitation of the architectural critics at both publications, the speculative proposals were developed in response to the public and critical opprobrium generated by the sanctioned master plans presented by the Lower Manhattan Development Corporation (LMDC) in July 2002, and energized the debate on the future of the 16-acre site and its adjacencies.

At the *Times*, Herbert Muschamp tapped a growing chorus of dissenters, led by a group of influential New York architects who were increasingly frustrated by the lack of ambition displayed by the official, developer-driven effort. In the summer of 2002, over a dozen established and ascendant "star shops" got together to hack out what Muschamp describes as a "study project." Frederic Schwartz—who helped direct the ill-fated Westway State Park development while at Venturi, Scott Brown & Associates twenty years ago—was asked to draft a plan that expanded the locus of redevelopment beyond the World Trade Center to encompass a dense triangle formed by West, Church and Chambers streets, with Battery Park at its apex. The scheme proposed to leave most of Ground Zero a memorial park and transit hub, redistributing sixteen acres of commercial and residential space along a 13-block stretch of West Street reclaimed from a six-lane highway. Flanked on one side by a continuous park, the lots along Schwartz's West Street Promenade were then parceled out to the study participants—which apart from the original conclave of Peter Eisenman, Richard Meier, Steven Holl, Charles Gwathmey, and engineer Guy Nordenson, also included Rem Koolhaas, Zaha Hadid, Rafael Viñoly, Maya Lin, Enrique Norten, Lindy Roy, Stephen Cassell, Adam Yarinsky, Hank Koning, Julie Eizenberg, Alexander Gorlin, Peter De Pasquale, Todd Fouser, Reuben Jorsling, Sean Tracy, and David Rockwell.

Design Study:
Port Authority of New York and New Jersey
Lower Manhattan Development Corporation

Joseph Giovannini, at *New York* magazine, elected to have each of the seven practices he approached create an individual, comprehensive vision for the entire site. Zaha Hadid, Thom Mayne of Morphosis, William Pedersen of Kohn Pedersen Fox, Peter Eisenman, Wolf Prix of Coop Himmelb(l)au, Carlos Zapata of Zapata + Wood, and Lebbeus Woods all suggested monumental gestures, connected to earth and water by a diversity of pedestrian-friendly uses. Prescribed by Giovannini as "curative doses of the beautiful, poetic and the sublime," the soaring structures at the heart of nearly all the designs give form to the creative energies latent in the site.

Pages 336-337

09. *New York Times Magazine:*
Site plan by Frederic Schwartz of West Street Promenade. Areas shaded in yellow denote proposed building sites, and parkland is indicated in green.

10. *New York Times Magazine:*
Office buildings proposed by Eisenman Architects for the largest parcel on West Street, bordered to the south by Liberty Street, to the north by Vesey Street, and to the east by the footprints of the World Trade Center towers.

11. *New York Times Magazine:*
View to north of West Street, with a residential tower by Zaha Hadid overlooking the Statue of Liberty ferry landing.

12. *New York:*
A 1,300-foot communications tower dominates the sprawling plan devised by Thom Mayne of Morphosis.

13. *New York:*
West Street and WTC site redevelopment by William Pedersen of Kohn Pedersen Fox. The tower Pedersen designed rises 2,001 feet over the city.

14. *New York:*
The linked towers of Zaha Hadid's scheme overlook an enormous multilevel podium.

The Port Authority of New York and New Jersey and the Lower Manhattan Development Corporation (LMDC)—the entity chartered by New York City and New York State in November 30, 2001 to oversee the rebuilding of the World Trade Center site—issued a joint Request for Proposal (RFP) for a phased "Integrated Urban Design and Transportation Study" on April 23, 2002. The fifteen teams that tendered submissions were whittled down to a limited pool of six Manhattan-based practices. Selecting from a list that included Davis Brody Bond, Ehrenkrantz Eckstut & Kuhn, Fox & Fowle, Kohn Pedersen Fox, and Robert A.M. Stern Architects, the planning commission was awarded to Beyer Blinder Belle, known chiefly for the revitalization of Grand Central Terminal (1999).

The six land-use proposals that Beyer Blinder Belle—in association with Parsons Brinckerhoff and eleven other consultants—presented on July 16, 2002 rigidly interpreted a narrow brief devised by the stakeholders to restore 11 million square-feet of office program and 1.2 million square-feet of hotel and retail use, clustered around a permanent memorial and a new transportation hub. Roundly criticized as anemic, the Phase I schemes endured a spectacularly harsh public reception at a "Listening to the City" event held at the Jacob. K Javits Center four days later.

Severely chastened, LMDC and the Port Authority floated a new RFP for a "design study" on August 19, 2002. Now open to international firms, the revised competition guidelines stipulated the design of a landmark tower, new cultural amenities, a pedestrian connection along West Street to the ferry terminals, linked public spaces, a restoration of the street grid the original World Trade center displaced, and an apparent reduction in the commercial program. Mandating ample space for a future, permanent memorial, the new guidelines also proscribed commercial development on top of the footprints formerly occupied by the twin towers.

Seven finalist teams were selected from nearly 400 applicants on September 26, 2002. Nine new plans were announced at a press conference held inside the rebuilt Winter Garden at the World Financial Center on December 18, 2002. "Memory Foundations," the scheme submitted by the Berlin-based firm of American architect Daniel Libeskind was selected six weeks later, on February 4, 2003.

Pages 338-343

15. - 16. Richard Meier & Partners Architects, Eisenman Architects, Gwathmey Siegel & Associates, and Steven Holl Architects.

17. - 21. United Architects:
Foreign Office Architects, Greg Lynn FORM, Kevin Kennon Architect, Reiser + Umemoto RUR Architecture, UN Studio, and Imaginary Forces.

22. Foster and Partners.

23. - 24. Skidmore, Owings & Merrill, Kazuyo Sejima + Ryue Nishizawa / SANAA, Michael Maltzan Architecture, Field Operations, Tom Leader Studio, Iñigo Manglano-Ovalle, Rita McBride, Jessica Stockholder, and Elyn Zimmerman.

25. - 27. THINK Design:
Shigeru Ban, Frederic Schwartz, Ken Smith, and Rafael Viñoly. THINK presented three schemes—Sky Park (fig. 25), Great Hall (fig. 26) and World Cultural Center—during the LMDC's December 18, 2002 press conference.

28. - 29. Studio Daniel Libeskind:
"Memory Foundations."

06.

07.

08.

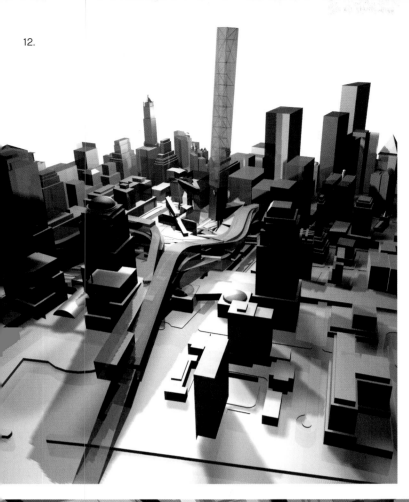

12.

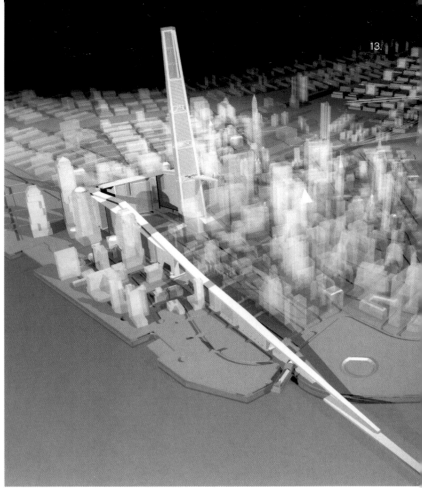

13.

14.

15.

16.

17.

18.

19.

20.

21.

22

23.

24.

TRAIN IS DEPARTING FROM TRACK #24 AT 1:15 ALL PASSENGERS PLEASE TRAIN3 :08 Y   E DEPARTING FROM TRACK #3 AT 1:20   ALL PASSENGERS PLEASE - TRAIN #9 FROM NEW YORK TO PHILADELPHIA   E DEPARTING FROM TRACK 2 TRAIN 24 WILL BE DEPAR

25.

26.

27.

Rector Street Bridge

Rector and West streets
SHoP
199X-2001

02.

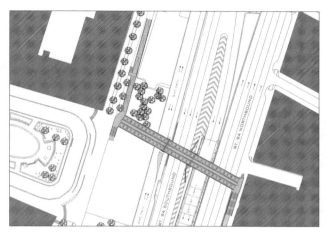

03.

04.

This pedestrian bridge is the first public infrastructure erected in the vicinity of the World Trade Center site after the events of September 11, 2001. The temporary walkway— spanning 230 feet across—reconnects Battery Park City and the World Financial Center to the rest of Lower Manhattan over West Street, a six-lane highway. West Street was the access route for all emergency vehicles and heavy-payload trucks in and out of Ground Zero in the aftermath of the attacks; minimal disruption to essential work done at the site was an important factor in the construction sequence.

The Battery Park City Authority brought in SHoP as designer and coordinator for the project. The architects had to mediate between the requirements of Battery Park City, the World Financial Center, the New York State Department of Transportation and the individual concerns of many other city, state and federal actors in producing a viable scheme on time and within the $3.5 million allotted by the Federal Emergency Management Agency.

The superstructure is a prefabricated galvanized steel box truss system. A steel roof truss system wraps around the walkway, providing shelter and cladding the north and south elevations. Gaps between the exterior panels permit occasional views out to the street and allow natural light to filter through during the day. Conversely, lamps embedded into the floor of the bridge illuminate the walkway at night, allowing light to escape through the porous exterior wall surfaces. The addition of light planks along the ramp and stair risers mark the direction of foot traffic, leading pedestrians safely across West Street.

01. View looking east.

02. Locator plan showing proximity to Ground Zero.

03. In plan, the 230-foot bridge forms a right angle with a 170-foot access ramp on the Battery Park City side.

04. South elevation.

05.

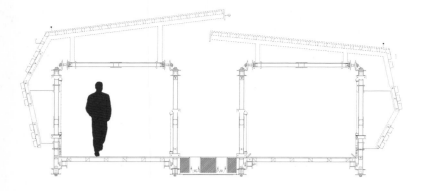

05. Section through bridge looking west.

06. View of light bars embedded into pavement.

07. Tolerances between the exterior steel panels
allow sunlight to filter in.

08. - 09. Entry sequence along Battery Park City.

Illustration Credits

Peter Aaron / Esto, 142, 158 (fig. 02), 264-265

Fabien Baron, 56-59

Richard Barnes, 86 (fig. 02), 86 (fig. 03), 89-91

Richard Barnes / Esto, 249-250

Base, 94 (fig. 04-09)

Doug Baz / Courtesy of Douglas Thompson, 106, 108-109

Lydia Gould Bessler, 6 (fig. 01), 66, 110, 274 (fig. 07)

Nicholas Borel, 9 (fig. 09), 224, 226-229

Melinda Buie, 114 (figs. 02-03)

Courtesy of Cheim & Read, 114 (fig. 01)

Whitney Cox, 316-317

Richard Davies, 104-105

H. G. Esch, 180, 183

Elizabeth Felicella / Copyright, The Museum of Modern Art, 286, 289, 290 (fig. 10)

Denis Finnin / AMNH, 246, 252

Jeff Goldberg / Esto, 120, (fig. 01-03), 123 (fig. 09-11), 162, 164-165, 282-285, 308, 310 (fig. 05-06),

Eric Höweler, 8 (fig. 04), 116

Eduard Hueber / Arch Photo, 24-25

David Joseph, 50-53, 176, 178-179, 220, 222-223, 294, 295 (fig. 06),

Keith Kaseman, 295 (fig. 07)

Philip Kelly / Courtesy of ROY, 298

Michael Kleinberg, 99

Elliot Kaufman, 10 (fig. 12), 168-170, 172-175

Seong Kwon, 345 (fig. 04), 346 (fig. 08)

Eric Liangel / Courtesy of Vitra, 87 (fig. 07), 88

Armin Linke / Courtesy of OMA, 64 (fig. 09)

Thomas Loof, 132, 135

Karen Ludlam, 344, 346 (figs. 06-07), 347

Jonathan Mallie / Courtesy of SHoP, 292 (fig. 02)

Peter Mauss / Esto, 270-272, 275

Michael Moran, 8 (fig. 06), 10 (fig. 11), 10 (fig. 13), 22-23, 48 (fig. 04), 60, 74, 76-77, 96-98, 124, 126-129, 198, 200-203, 208, 210-214, 216-219, 240, 242-245, 252, 254-255, 292 (figs. 01, 03),

John Morrison / Courtesy of Polshek Partnership, 134

Katherine Newbegin, 34-35, 69, 85

NOAA, 345 (fig. 02)

Tomio Ohashi, 136, 138-139

Richard Payne, 194

Matthu Placek, 118-119

Robert Polidori, 18

Tom Powell, 88

Gernot Reither / Courtesy of ROY, 296

Courtesy Ian Schrager Hotels / Full Picture, 232-235

Jan Staller, 300 (fig. 04), 302

David Sundberg / Esto, 166 (fig. 05), 256-259, 278, 280 (figs. 04-05), 281, (figs. 04-05)

Thomas Tsang, 94 (fig. 01-03)

Eric van den Brulle / Copyright, The Museum of Modern Art, 288, 290 (fig. 09)

Albert Vecerka / Esto, 268 (fig. 01)

Paul Warchol, 10 (fig. 10), 28-31, 38-40, 46, 48 (fig. 03), 49, 54-55, 62-63, 72-73, 78-79, 80 (fig. 06), 81, 154,156-157, 190-191,196-197, 260, 262-263, 311

Heidi Werner / Courtesy of ROY, 86 (fig. 04)

Harry Zernike, 112

Unless otherwise indicated, all drawings and renderings appear courtesy of the architects.

Throughout this publication, Japanese names follow the Western convention in which the given name precedes the family name. This order is reversed only in cases where the name is a trademark.

Acknowledgments

New New York would not have been possible without the involvement of many talented individuals. I would first like to extend my appreciation to the architects, the photographers and the other creative professionals who contributed visual, graphic and textual information. Their toil gave form and content to this book.

I am indebted to the steadfast patronage of my editors, David Morton and Stephen Case, and greatly benefited from their insight and guidance. I would also like to acknowledge the editorial assistance and support provided by the staff at Rizzoli International Publications, and by Joseph Giovannini, Eric Höweler, Ellen Cohen, Laura Crescimano, Sara Moss, Kam Lee, Thomas Tsang, Edward Ng, Jacob Tilove, and Hanae Kuramochi. It was a pleasure to have worked with all of you.

The design and editorial support provided by Eugene Lee and Michael Aneiro was particularly invaluable. Their twinned effort—exerted throughout an unremitting schedule—was nothing short of miraculous. Special thanks go out to Zetima.

New New York is dedicated to all the alumni from Central Park East, Brooklyn Tech, Collegiate, RFK, Gompers, UNIS, Horace Mann, Humanities, Spence, Monsignor Farrell, The Friends School, Lower East Side Prep, Xavierian Brooklyn, and Hunter High School, who lent a hand in its creation— or else were just hanging around.

And the city was pure gold, like unto clear glass.

Ian Luna

Any copy of this book issued by the publisher as a paperback is sold
subject to the condition that it shall not by way of trade or otherwise
be lent, resold, hired out or otherwise circulated without the publisher's prior
consent in any form of binding or cover other than that in which
it is published and without a similar condition including these words
being imposed on a subsequent purchaser.

First published in the United Kingdom in 2003
by Thames & Hudson Ltd, 181A High Holborn,
London WC1V 7QX

www.thamesandhudson.com

© 2003 Rizzoli International Publications Inc.

All Rights Reserved. No part of this publication may be reproduced
or transmitted in any form or by any means, electronic or mechanical, including
photocopy, recording or any other information storage and retrieval system,
without prior permission in writing from the publisher.

British Library Cataloguing-in-Publication Data
A catalogue record for this book is available from the British Library

ISBN 0-500-284547

Printed and bound in Belgium

U.W.E.L. LEARNING RESOURCES